Echoes of His Heart

DEBBIE ANDREWS SMITH

KW
Kingdom Winds
Publishing

*Scripture quotations are taken from the Holy Bible, New Living Translation,
copyright ©1996, 2004, 2015 by Tyndale House Foundation. Used by per-
mission of Tyndale House Publishers, Inc., Carol Stream, Illinois 60188. All
rights reserved.*

First Edition, 2018.

ISBN 10: 0998010545

ISBN 13: 9780998010540

Cover design by Gloria Biggers. Book design by Dawn King.

Published by Kingdom Winds Publishing.

www.kingdomwinds.com

publishing@kingdomwinds.com

The views expressed in this book are not necessarily those of the publisher.

Printed in the United States of America

" Whether you feel hurting in your heart or joy in your life, the verses in Echoes of His Heart will touch your spirit with meaningful promises of God. Written in a style easy to read and followed by scriptural passages supporting each thought, this book offers a beneficial beginning to your morning or a thoughtful end to your day. "

-The Reverend Dr. David L. Haun

Dedication

Firstly, I dedicate this book to the Author of my life and Co-Author of this book. Without Him, I am nothing. He gives me the breath I breathe and the day in which to take each breath. He's given me every ability and positive characteristic of who I am. Everything I love comes directly from Him. This is all for the glory of the Holy Trinity; the Father, the Son, and the Holy Spirit!

Secondly, I dedicate this to all those who are in deep despair but discover hope. To those who've never felt they could be forgiven but find peace and assurance in the forgiveness and sacrifice of Jesus Christ. To those who receive God's genuine love for the first time and realize that their emptiness is only filled by His presence. To those who cherish that they are loved sons and daughters of the Living God and live according to His commands. To those who call upon the Lord for strength, acknowledge Him daily, and give Him praise. To those who stop using His holy name in vain and for those who begin to love instead of continuing to hate. To those who cherish and choose the gift of life. To those who realize that reading the Bible is a privilege and not a chore. To those who repent of their ways and whose souls are saved. To those who realize that God is great, and that inviting Jesus into their lives is the best decision that they could ever make.

My Encounter with the Divine

It was on a morning walk in the fall of 2011 that I was given the honor and privilege of hearing God Almighty speak. Among many things, I was praying for a dear couple to be blessed. Their passion in sharing the Good News and the love of Jesus Christ was very moving to me. As I continued walking, I was praying for confidence to be more outspoken about my faith so that I, too, might be used in leading souls to our Lord and Savior, Jesus Christ. Much to my surprise, I was overcome by the Spirit of God and heard the most powerful and loving voice from above. He said, "Debbie, I hear you, and they will be blessed because saving souls is what it's all about. Don't worry; you'll find your own way to speak about Me."

That morning was the first time I heard the undeniable and audible voice of God, so I was shocked and in awe to say the very least. The same voice who created the world and everything in it spoke to me with an immediate response to a prayer I just prayed. I was addressed by name, told that my prayers were heard, and given a promise that blessings would come. Although I wasn't given a clue as to what my own way would be, I was quite certain that the Lord was referring to a very specific way that I'd speak.

It seemed as though time stood still while God's words were being spoken. Nothing else surrounding me had a chance to compete. My heart was beating with such force it felt like God's heartbeat was in rhythm with mine. His presence was so tangible and so strong that it literally took my breath away. I couldn't contain the power of His presence and can fully appreciate why this encounter was kept so brief. These moments were the most intense moments imaginable, but because I knew without a doubt that my God was ever so close, fear didn't stand a chance. I was totally surrounded and protected by the Lord's presence and made to feel like I was being given His undivided attention. I heard His voice, felt His heartbeat, and received prophecy all at the same time! I like to refer to this experience as the Holy Trifecta, and I welcome any aspect of this any day—morning, noon, or night. God is beyond amazing! I was praying for others to be blessed, and the Lord turns around and blesses me. His imprint and the memory of that day is forever embedded on my heart. It was like a baptism of His love and definitely the highlight of my life. I got a taste of what it feels like to become one with the Lord. There was such peace and a feeling of wholeness. I didn't want it to end and can only imagine what lies ahead.

The Mystery is Solved

I always thought it would be neat to write a book, especially one of short stories, but had no idea what the content would be or if I even had the ability to do so. The iPad I received as a birthday gift in 2012 changed that dream into a reality, bringing my desire full circle. I can definitely see the Lord's hand in it; He even topped it off with a shiny red bow! I had no idea as to what I would ever do with such a device, but God sure did. All I wanted to do was write, and in one way or another, it had to do with Him. Up to that point, I had written a dozen or so family-oriented poems over a twenty-five-year period. I started sharing some of my new material with family and friends and was encouraged to get them published. But it wasn't until one of my sons told me that my writing was a gift from God that He would want me to share that revelation set in, and the mystery was solved. The words that I had wondered about since the day they were spoken immediately returned to me, and I finally knew what my own way would be. The joining of the two was a definite lightbulb moment and a day I'll never forget. The camouflage was removed, and I was finally able to see what was in front of me all along.

The book I'd dreamed of writing came to fruition that day. God knows my heart and has been nurturing me my entire life for such a time as this. My dabbling with what I like to refer to as *floetry has turned into a passion that enables me to convey Scriptural truths in a very short story. It's truly the work of *the Holy Spirit flowing and working within me, which in turn, flows from my heart and soul to another. Not only has God given me an imagination, empathy, compassion, and the ability to write; He's enabled me to incorporate His truths in the midst of it. The Lord sure does work in mysterious ways. Philippians 2:13 resonates with me, "For God is working in you, giving you the desire and the power to do what pleases him."

My Leap of Faith

I am not a Bible scholar by any means, but what I know for sure is this: Not only is God alive—He hears, and He speaks! I never imagined that I would be doing anything of this magnitude, as this is way bigger than I am and totally out of my comfort zone. Writing about God in any way wasn't anything that ever crossed my mind. But God thinks otherwise, and who am I to question Him about anything? He believes in me, and that's all the encouragement that I need. This is my giant leap of faith in addition to my obedience to my King.

I'm very grateful that I was only given a piece of the puzzle on my morning walk. God knew full well that I was not ready to hear what He didn't reveal on that phenomenal day. I would have doubted my capability, resulting in doubting Him. He gave me time to do some writing so there would be no question that I was capable of the assignment ahead.

I'm still in awe that the Lord deliberately took time from His day and made a definite point to allow me to feel His presence and hear what He had to day. I believe this divine assignment was spoken into existence, or conceived, if you will, at that very moment. It's gone through the developmental stages a word at a time, and now this book is a testimony of my faith and my contribution and tribute to my God, the God of Creation. It's a little legacy I leave behind that could also very well define my higher purpose in life.

I am beyond honored that God has entrusted and chosen me for this unique and incredible journey with and for Him. Just as Queen Esther spoke up, resulting in many lives being spared, if anything I've written can bring one wanderer back or lead one soul to Jesus Christ, then this book will have achieved its purpose. Jesus is the Truth, the Life, and the Way. He is not a secret, and His Good News is very much meant to be shared.

I truly feel like the most privileged little girl who was asked to share her lunch in hopes that it may be blessed and multiplied to nourish and strengthen souls. I find it comforting that my name in Hebrew means bee. There would be no greater honor than to pollinate hearts and souls for the Kingdom of God.

In Him,

Debbie Andrews Smith

May the words of my mouth and the meditation of my heart be pleasing to you, O Lord, my rock and my redeemer.

Psalm 19:14

Contents

Alive

I was looking in all the wrong places
I was chasing all the wrong things
My self-centered life was eroding away
I was a lost soul until the most incredible day

I couldn't do it without Jesus any longer
I repented of my past and surrendered all
Rock bottom was an eye-opening blessing for me
I gave praise to the Lord while I was on my knees

I asked for His forgiveness and for the first time felt—free
A heavy weight was lifted; I could finally breathe
My old desires aren't important anymore
They don't fit in with the new me

I have Jesus! His love is written all over my face
He loves me so much that He covered my shame
I have nothing but joy knowing Jesus paid for my sins
I'm no longer running away, but running straight to Him

It wasn't until I submitted that I felt so alive
and realized how dead I'd been inside
I have a clean slate, I'm reborn, I'm changed
Thank You, Lord Jesus, for removing my chains

My heavy weights are gone
I can finally and freely breathe
I'm alive for the very first time
The Holy Spirit is alive in me!

Humans can reproduce only human life, but the Holy Spirit gives birth to spiritual life.
John 3:6

Always Waiting for Me

I don't need a telephone, Skype, or GPS
I don't need to prepare for a long-dreaded trip
I don't have to brush my teeth or even fix my hair
I don't need the perfect outfit or have to climb the stairs

I don't have to go anywhere to find You, Lord
You're always waiting for me—Anytime, night or day
You're always waiting at Your throne of grace

I come into Your presence—
Grateful, remorseful, and truly repentant
Not wanting to live the same as before
Not wanting to live without *You*, Dear Lord

Thank You for being only a thought or prayer away
and for hearing every word that I'll ever say or pray
Could that be why You never slumber or sleep?
Is it because, You're always *waiting* for me?

So let us come boldly to the throne of our gracious God. There we will receive his mercy, and we will find grace to help us when we need it most.

Hebrews 4:16

Antidote

Sin is a toxin that pollutes our entire being
It fills us with selfishness, pride, and greed
It contaminates with unforgiveness and resentment
It invades in anger, revenge, jealousy, and deceit

These poisons don't mix well with our spirits
They don't mix well with our souls
But there is a pure remedy, a cure, and a hope
Detoxing with Jesus is the sure antidote

Jesus purifies the deadly poisons within
as He turns our poor reflections
into a pure reflection of Him

Jesus fills us with the fruit of His Spirit
He fills us with love, joy, peace, patience, and kindness
With goodness, faithfulness, gentleness, and self-control

He fills us with forgiveness
He fills us with selflessness and hope
If you need to get rid of toxins
Jesus is the Antidote!

But the Holy Spirit produces this kind of fruit in our lives: love, joy, peace, patience, kindness, goodness, faithfulness, gentleness, and self-control. There is no law against these things!

Galatians 5:22-23

Are You Willing?

We won't experience many things
if we don't spend time with our Lord
How much time do you willingly give
to the One who sacrificed His life for yours?

Is going to church on Sunday morning
and saying meal and bedtime prayers enough?
It may appease us, but does it please the Lord?
It's definitely a start, but I believe He deserves more

Do you acknowledge the Lord when you awake?
Do you include Him in projects throughout your day?
Do you praise Him for who He is and always will be?
Do you thank Him for the breath you currently breathe?

Is reading His inspired Word part of your routine?
Do you thank Him for the birds that beautifully sing?
Do you thank Him for the mercy and grace He bestows?
Do you mention His greatness in places you go?

Do you thank God for the blessings He daily gives?
Do you share with others that Jesus died for our sins?
Do you willingly set time aside for just you and Him?
Do you willingly omit something you know He forbids?

How much time do you willingly give
to the One who gave His life for yours?
Are you willing to give Him more today
than you gave Him the day before?

Let all that I am praise the Lord; with my whole heart, I will praise his holy name. Let all that I am praise the Lord; may I never forget the good things he does for me. He forgives all my sins and heals all my diseases. He redeems me from death and crowns me with love and tender mercies.

Psalm 103:1-4

Arise

Arise, My Love, Arise!
These words were spoken
by God the Father to His Son
He also speaks these words to us

We, too, can be resurrected
We can be awakened from an empty life
From a life where we weren't living for Christ

If we don't surrender our hearts, our souls, and our minds
We're living a life of suffocation—We're buried alive
The stone is sealed until our desires are removed
A life with the Lord is how we're renewed

Jesus can't shine in us for all to see
until we live like He is our everything
Jesus gave us an example by which to live
He was selfless and loving—He taught to forgive

If we are the opposite of what Jesus is
we have some things we need to change
Rid the things that need not remain
Leave them behind in the cold, dark grave

Show the One who paid your price
how much you appreciate His sacrifice
Wake up! Arise! Live your life for Jesus Christ!
Nothing is more fulfilling than His Spirit living inside

Now may the God of peace – who brought up from the dead our Lord Jesus, the great Shepherd of the sheep, and ratified an eternal covenant with his blood— may he equip you with all you need for doing his will. May he produce in you, through the power of Jesus Christ, every good thing that is pleasing to him. All glory to him forever and ever! Amen.

Hebrews 13:20-21

Armor of God

We're overcomers if we so choose
With God on our side we'll never lose
We walk in confidence, in peace, and in truth
when our hope is in Jesus and in His Wonderful News

Life takes on new meaning and won't be lived in a fog
when we know whose we are and to whom we belong
We hold the power to detect all things that don't align
as darkness has no business in the Kingdom of Light

Our spiritual eyes illuminate the enemy in our midst
as wisdom and discernment expose every deceptive trick
Each lie planted is uprooted by the purity of truth and love
We've been equipped with nothing but the best from above

The infallible Word of God is precise in every way
Nothing holds a candle to the power it displays
The truth of these sacred writings puts evil in its place
as Scripture memorization is one of our greatest aids

Our faith is a mighty force field
It's our shield against the fiery spears
Darkness tries but his plans won't adhere
Evil is exposed when the Truth is held near

Our loving Father guards us with armor for each fight
and has given us the ability to destroy the father of lies
Together with God's presence, we spoil every evil scheme
and in doing so, we also, give praise to the Almighty King

For we are ... fighting against evil rulers ... of the unseen world ... put on ... God's armor ... the belt of truth and the body armor of God's righteousness. For shoes, put on the peace that comes from the Good News ... hold up the shield of faith to stop the fiery arrows of the devil. Put on salvation as your helmet, and take the sword of the Spirit, which is the word of God.

Ephesians 6:12-17

Barriers

They see my size and the color of my eyes
My gender, my race; things I can't disguise
My outdated wardrobe, my scars, and tattoos
They see my past that You've already renewed

Barriers are kept; they've taken a stance
I'm not given a chance; they barely glance
It's a crushing feeling to be rejected and scorned
but no one knows this better than You, my Lord

You don't see me as less than a fraction
You see my heart, my love, and compassion
You see me as Your child just as You do them
In You, I am complete—You hold me in Your hand

This discrimination will never part
until the Golden Rule is etched in our hearts
If we don't obey the commands God gives
there is no chance to remedy any of this

I won't dwell on things that others say or think
I'll savor Your thoughts and the way You look at me
I pray for repentance for a nation that is plagued
If only we'd say nothing in replace of words of hate

Thank You, Lord Jesus
for loving every gender, party, and race
I pray that it's in You and You alone
that we model and embrace

If anyone claims, "I am living in the light," but hates a fellow believer, that person is still living in darkness.

1 John 2:9

My dear brothers and sisters, how can you claim to have faith in our glorious Lord Jesus Christ if you favor some people over others?

James 2:1

Blink of an Eye

I wasn't living for the Lord
It's evident by the life I've lived
I'm ashamed and disappointed
and have more than many regrets

I was selfishly in "me" mode
I was restless and incomplete
but this new version of who I am
is the person I've longed to be

I invited Jesus into my heart
His Spirit is now my Guide
I had no idea I could be so full
yet so light at the same time

I've repented and asked for forgiveness
I thank Jesus for cleansing my stains
He's erased each one from His memory
He's removed the ball and chain

I have the Lord and His forgiveness—
Two treasures I desperately needed
I was so empty; but not anymore
Jesus Christ is my Savior and Lord

This life will be gone in the blink of an eye
A life without Christ is like life without light
His truth brings peace—His news redeems
I pray you, too, know Jesus as Savior and King

In him lie hidden all the treasures of wisdom and knowledge. I am telling you this so no one will deceive you with well-crafted arguments.

Colossians 2:3-4

Book of Life

You are chosen because you love Him
and of Him you are not ashamed
Your name is written in the Book of Life
and announced on the most sacred of days

Can you even begin to imagine
what that day will be like?
You'll be rewarded for loving Jesus
and receive the Crown of Life

You'll be standing in front of God Himself
the Creator of the World and all it contains
and in front of everyone and everything
your Savior calls your name

I can only imagine the thrill of this day
except for those who may hear, "Take them away—
Their name's not here; there's a blank space on the page"
I couldn't bear hearing that my name's been erased

If you can imagine such words being spoken to you
there's no time like the present to start living anew
Jesus sacrificed His life to erase our stains, not our name
I pray that you choose Jesus, as He is the only Way!

"All who are victorious will be clothed in white. I will never erase their names from the Book of Life, but I will announce before my Father and his angels that they are mine."

Revelation 3:5

God blesses those who patiently endure testing and temptation. Afterward they will receive the crown of life that God has promised to those who love him.

James 1:12

Broken

I'm broken, Lord—I've had a great fall
There are so many pieces—I've made such a mess
You're the only One who can put me together again

Nothing and no one else will do
I need the King of Kings—I need You
You know where all the pieces belong
and what doesn't need to be replaced

Please forgive me, Dear Lord
for not living in line with Your ways
I reflect on my past and see so much waste
I can't go back, but I can sure give You praise

You are the Potter who gave me new life
the day I repented and accepted You as my Guide
The touch of Your hands absorbed deep in my soul
I'm no longer broken—I'm a brand-new mold

I'm so sorry; I apologize for treating You as a chore
I don't want to neglect or disrespect You anymore
I want to live the rest of my life, living for You
You are fascinating and hold so much truth

I'm a living testimony of Your love and Your grace
You put me together, and I'll never be the same
I'm no longer broken—I'm completely whole
Thank You, Lord God, for saving my soul!

The sacrifice you desire is a broken spirit. You will not reject a broken and repentant heart, O God.

Psalm 51:17

"And what do you benefit if you gain the whole world but lose your own soul? Is anything worth more than your soul?"

Mark 8:36

Bucket List

I'm the Dad; it's my job to provide
I excelled in providing materialism
We traveled and had fun, but
the Lord wasn't present in our lives

He's all I think about now
I saw Him in all His glory
sitting at the right hand of God
with beauty all around

I was on the outside looking in
My wife and kids were with me
We had absolutely everything
except our much-needed salvation

"I'm really scared, Daddy—When can we leave?"
"I'm sorry, Honey, we can't—We lost our chance
This is the consequence for rejecting our King
This is where our family will spend eternity"

I woke up and immediately got on my knees
and thanked God for sending this timely dream
I accepted Jesus as my Savior that night
We all started living our lives for Jesus Christ

It was much more fulfilling than ever before
My dream saved our lives, Thank You, Lord!
If we deny Jesus in this life, He'll deny us in the next
Is accepting and living for Jesus Christ on your *bucket list*?

"Everyone who acknowledges me publicly here on earth, I will also acknowledge before my Father in heaven. But everyone who denies me here on earth, I will also deny before my Father in heaven."

Matthew 10:32-33

Calm This Storm in Me

I call upon You, Wonderful Counselor
I need You, Prince of Peace
My Protector, my Healer, my Comforter
Please calm this storm in me

I need some time, and I need it with You
You're the only One who truly renews
You replace my anxiety with abundant gifts
You listen and guide—You nurture and lift

Thank You for being my anchor
and rescuing me from the raging sea
You've stilled the ferocious waves
into a very peaceful stream

Thank You for being my counselor
and for being my inner peace
Thank You for being my comforter
and for calming this storm in me

I can't thank You enough for being by my side
and for hearing my calls and my cries
Your love, O Lord, will never subside
It's as deep as it is wide

The storm has ceased; the course has changed
There is such power in Your mighty names
You are my protector, my healer, and my peace
You possess everything that I'll ever need

Jesus responded, "Why are you afraid? You have so little faith!" Then he got up and rebuked the wind and waves, and suddenly there was a great calm. The disciples were amazed. "Who is this man?" they asked. "Even the winds and waves obey him!"

Matthew 8:26-27

The Carpenter of Galilee

I know a builder that's in great demand
There is none finer in the entire land
He has vision beyond what any man sees
as each creation is His grand masterpiece

You'll be in awe—He takes first place
He's filled with integrity, mercy, and grace
His artistic abilities and designs are divine
Everything He creates uniquely combines

He's a builder you'll thank and daily praise
Once you've met Him, you'll never be the same
He's a miracle worker, the greatest there is
He beautifully intertwines your life into His

He cares so much that He places a remembrance within
a Guide that keeps you close and connected to Him
He also leaves a manual containing absolute truth
It's flawless and perfect, written especially for you

All who choose Him choose a lifetime guarantee
He pays your debt in full; there are no hidden fees
His name is Jesus if you've never heard or care to know
This Carpenter of Galilee took the nails to save your soul

His holy body was sacrificed out of His amazing love
Every sin you've ever committed is washed by His holy blood
If you've never given your heart to Jesus, today can be that day
What a Savior we have in Jesus; your estate is a prayer away

"Unless the LORD builds a house, the work of the builders is wasted. Unless the LORD protects a city, guarding it with sentries will do no good."

Psalm 127:1

Cast Your Cares

Cast your cares and burdens on the Lord
Don't live a life that's misconstrued
Jesus longs to help us with our burdens
He wants them to be removed

Jesus wants us to be set free
He doesn't want anyone to be in chains
He's the Physician who heals all wounds
He alleviates our pain and shame

Jesus is so selfless that He died for our sins
and He still wants us to cast our cares upon Him
Jesus is our strength when we are hopeless and weak
We are encouraged to present our troubles to our King

His perfect love replaces each weight we opt to cast
Jesus fills up the spaces we didn't even know we had
Tell Him what's bothering you; give it to Him straight
Tell Him about all your burdens that are in the way

Fall on your knees, and praise the Lord Most High
Thank Him for hearing your heart when it cries
Thank Him for His love and for His sacrifice
Thank Him for always being by your side

We are so fortunate to call upon our holy God
whose love for us is incomprehensible
There are a lot of things we can live without
but His presence is indispensable!

Give your burdens to the Lord, and he will take care of you. He will not permit the godly to slip and fall.

Psalm 55:22

Cherish

We can all be replaced
in one way or another
on this earth on which we live

This doesn't apply in the eyes of God
There is only one you and one me
We're irreplaceable to Him

We are His children
He created us—He loves us
We are cherished

Can you imagine the Lord
waiting for the day for us to realize
that what we long for is Him?

Next week
Two more minutes
One second remaining

Heaven rejoices when a sinner repents
The Lord doesn't want any of us to perish
Does your life reflect that Jesus is someone you cherish?

Long ago the Lord said to Israel: "I have loved you, my people, with an everlasting love. With unfailing love I have drawn you to myself."

Jeremiah 31:3

"In the same way, there is joy in the presence of God's angels when even one sinner repents."

Luke 15:10

Choked Out

God fills each new day with blessings galore
We feed our flesh; our loving God we ignore

We inhale and ingest, polluting His temple
God is choked out with the things we assemble

Our thoughts, actions, and words we speak
Obsessions, extravagance, consuming greed

We're so self-absorbed, thinking only of us
Our indulgent desires and selfish lusts

The latest gadgets, upgrades, and fashions
Our day is filled with numerous distractions

Forgive us, Dear God, for replacing You
with worldly things that taint Your truth

I pray for awareness with each new day
and for thanksgiving and praise to be sent Your way

I pray that we'll give You more time than we have in the past
and direct our attention on what's important and will last

All night long I search for you; in the morning I earnestly seek you. For only when you come to judge the earth will people learn what is right.

Isaiah 26:9

Chosen Instrument

People didn't trust Saul
He wanted Christians dead
He wanted to destroy the church
expressing threats with every breath

He was eager to kill the Lord's followers
arresting all who call on His name
but Saul was God's chosen instrument
playing the tune that Jesus saves

He no longer did things contrary to his newfound belief
He turned over a new leaf after hearing Jesus speak
Saul shared about Christ's love, His mercy, and His grace
He spread nothing but truth to the entire human race

He taught the opposite of what he once taught
He began teaching that Jesus is indeed the Son of God
He no longer persecuted but spread the Good News
He was no longer confused about the King of the Jews

Saul, renamed Paul, had new identity in Christ
He was no longer blinded after seeing the light
As snakes shed their covering to produce new growth
scales fell from his eyes, and he was filled with the Holy Ghost

Each word and deed not said or done in love is a scale
We are called to love; it's a direct command, not a tale
If you have any scales of ungodliness that need to be removed
there's no time like the present for new management in you

He fell to the ground and heard a voice saying to him, "Saul! Saul! Why are you persecuting me?" "Who are you, lord?" Saul asked. And the voice replied, "I am Jesus, the one you are persecuting! Now get up and go into the city, and you will be told what you must do."

Acts 9:3-6

Clean Out Your Heart

Is there any darkness housed in your heart
taking up precious and valuable space?
Does it resurface from time to time
exposing its stench and ugly face?

If what we carry doesn't represent God
it's a direct indication of what needs to part
We choose to host treasure or piles of trash
Hosting God's presence creates beauty that lasts

Our hearts' locations are prime real estate
They're best inhabited when God's love fills this space
When we love like Him and have compassion like His
our hearts will be full of things that He freely gives

It won't beat with division, racism, or pride
Or with resentment or anger, or immorality or lies
Or with bitterness or hatred, or offenses or blame
Or with unforgiveness, control, fear, doubt, or shame

Hatred and lies are replaced with love and truth
Forgiving as God forgives is what we'll also choose
We repent, confess, trust in Him, and seek peace
We pray for those who are causing us grief

Our hearts determine the paths that we'll take
and need to be guarded so Godly choices are made
I pray for a pure heart where the love of God is stored
and a clear conscience to worship my Lord

Point out anything in me that offends you, and lead me along the path of everlasting life.
Psalm 139:24

The purpose of my instruction is that all believers would be filled with love that comes from a pure heart, a clear conscience, and genuine faith.
1 Timothy 1:5

Guard your heart above all else, for it determines the course of your life.
Proverbs 4:23

Cloud Nine

The state of complete euphoria
is commonly known as cloud nine
It's a feeling of great happiness
It's paradise; it's an intoxicating high

I have a vision of a cloud nine scene
An anticipated day showcasing the King
We're on the most amazing ride of our lives
as we're taken to the realm of Heaven's heights

The day is chosen
It's no longer unknown
The Lord is coming
down from His throne

A commanding shout and trumpet blast
announce that the day has come at last
By the power of God, the dead are raised
and caught up with Jesus on one majestic day

His day has arrived—No one can turn a blind eye
Jesus is in the air, taking us to everlasting life
We'll be riding in the clouds with God Most High
That's what I call a glorious cloud nine

Do you anticipate the coming of Jesus Christ?
Does living with Him forever bring you delight?
Are you looking forward to hearing the trumpet blast
and meeting the Lord in the air to be with Him at last?

For the Lord himself will come down from heaven … with the voice of the archangel, and with the trumpet call of God. First, the Christians who have died will rise … Then, we who are still alive … will be caught up in the clouds to meet the Lord in the air. Then we will be with the Lord forever.

1 Thessalonians 4:16-17

Completely Whole

I pray for healing in every aspect of your life
I pray for you to feel your worth in Jesus Christ
I pray for you to draw closer to Him with each new day
For He is whom we need for our health to be maintained

Don't ever doubt that you are worthy
Don't ever doubt that you are loved
Don't allow the past to rob your future
Put your trust in the One above

The Lord thinks very highly of *you*
He adores *you*—His love is immense
Please don't listen to voices that say otherwise
You are a treasure that's held close to His chest

His opinion of you is what matters
No one else knows all things
He loves, and He forgives
You're safe in the shelter of His wings

You'll never be free until you believe this is true
Dismiss all interference that tries to cloud this truth
If you don't love yourself, you'll never be whole
and be able to take back what the enemy stole

Take delight in each new day
Let the Joy of the Lord become your strength
Let His love saturate your heart, your mind, and soul
It's only then that you'll be completely whole

He will cover you with his feathers. He will shelter you with his wings. His faithful promises are your armor and protection.

Psalm 91:4

Confession

Our holy God hears our heartfelt confession
and in turn forgives us from our transgressions
What a treasure we have in this precious gift
We ask God for forgiveness, and He forgives

If you've never confessed to the Lord before
it's the most freeing experience you'll ever find
We all make mistakes, have regrets, and fall short
but God's mercy and grace cleanse and refine

Jesus is waiting for us to repent and turn to Him
With open arms, He takes us into His
He feels our remorse and absolves our sins
He washes away our ungodliness

Jesus doesn't hold grudges—He conveys loving words
He says, "You're Forgiven"—The two best words to be heard
He looks into your eyes and places a kiss on your face
then welcomes you home into His holy embrace

Jesus sends for the best and throws a grand feast
He shows that His love hasn't decreased in the least
He's so pleased you've come home and seen the light
that you're no longer wandering and safe in His sight

We needed a Savior; that's why Jesus came
He forgives all who confess and repent of their ways
Jesus wipes our slate clean—It's erased without a trace
We are cleansed by His sacrifice and blessed by His grace

Oh, what joy for those whose disobedience is forgiven, whose sins are put out of sight. Yes, what joy for those whose record the LORD has cleared of sin.

Romans 4:7-8

But if we confess our sins to him, he is faithful and just to forgive us our sins and to cleanse us from all wickedness.

1 John 1:9

Consequence

We suffer consequences when we make mistakes
What's the biggest mistake you've ever made?
Are you ashamed? Do you regret it?
Have you confessed? Have you repented?

If we don't love Jesus Christ
for who He is and for what He's done
we'll suffer the greatest consequence of all—
Eternal separation from the Father and the Son

We'll all see that Jesus is not a myth
He's very real—He is not a fantasy
Every knee will bend and tongue proclaim
that Jesus Christ is Lord and King

Is that a day you look forward to?
If not, do you have some soul-searching to do?
Are there first some things you need to change?
Are there some things you need to eliminate?

You'll never know how empty you were
until you allow Jesus to fill the void
Your soul will sing a brand-new song
You'll be totally overjoyed

Jesus is coming back unexpectedly
and He will judge us all respectively
Do you believe that these are true statements of faith?
Consequences are not fun when we make mistakes

For the Scriptures say, "'As surely as I live,' says the Lord, 'every knee will bend to me, and every tongue will confess and give praise to God.'"

Romans 14:11

Constrictor

Do you feel suffocated?
Is it hard for you to breathe?
Do you feel constricted?
Is it hard for you to sleep?

Are you angry, hurt, or bitter?
Are you negative beyond belief?
Are you fearful or always doubting?
Are you living a life of deceit?

Is something lurking around?
Is something eating at you?
Is there an unwelcome spirit
that has a grasp on you?

It's more than creepy but also very true
Serpents really can wrap themselves around you
Constrictors blend right in, waiting for their prey
anticipating the attack so they can take your life away

It's no laughing matter
The enemy wants to destroy your soul
It's very serious business, so he's on constant patrol
The adversary will do anything to gain and keep control

Sever his coils with the Sword of the Spirit
The Word of God is full of power and truth
Slash them so he can't continue to feed
In the name of Jesus, command him to leave!

Therefore, put on every piece of God's armor so you will be able to resist the enemy in the time of evil.

Ephesians 6:13

Covered

Jesus, the finest man that ever lived
suffered for crimes that weren't even His
He was brutally beaten—His skin torn to shreds
His entire body was covered in red

Jesus shed His blood to cover the sins of all mankind
He hung until the final sin was paid, and then He died
Jesus paid for every sin that you and I have ever made
He defeated sin and darkness—He defeated the grave

Jesus takes us from sin to holiness
from filthy rags to royal robes
His sacrifice enables us eternal life
with the Heavenliest of Hosts

Can you feel the love in His sacrifice?
Jesus became sin to cover yours and mine
He removed the penalty of sin, which was death
and enables us to be faultless in His eyes

Jesus Christ is our Savior and King
He takes our stains and washes them clean
Our sins are erased by the shedding of His blood
They were nailed to the cross in a labor of love

We're made right with God when we believe this is true
and when we believe this is true, our actions become new
Our loving God made a way for us to be whole
All praise to Jesus, the Lover of our souls

You were dead because of your sins and because your sinful nature was not yet cut away. Then God made you alive with Christ, for he forgave all our sins. He canceled the record of the charges against us and took it away by nailing it to the cross.

Colossians 2:13-14

The Dance

It enters our lives with a very quick step
It's a slick little fish, a sneaky one to catch
It hammers away at us until we believe
that wrong is right and it's cool to demean

It twists our thoughts and clouds our vision
It jerks us around until we change our decisions
It jives and then thrives on compromises made
as it encourages and validates desires that we crave

It's a snake whose aim is to inject deceit
Its venom is lethal; its poison runs deep
It sways and leads us into a life without hope
It wants us to feel unworthy, unloved, and alone

It's a pesky, little jitterbug
that tries its best to swing us high
into his world of immorality and lies
I praise God for exposing his toxic disguise

One step, two step, three step, four
I refuse to be hustled and permit him on my floor
A good swift jolt is what this force of evil needs
A boot scootin' boogie that brings him to his knees

It's time to celebrate; to twist and shout
Jesus is King; let there be no room for doubt
There will soon be a day when the waltz is performed
as this dance highlights our dance with the Mighty Lord!

"You have turned my mourning into joyful dancing. You have taken away my clothes of mourning and clothed me with joy, that I might sing praises to you and not be silent. O Lord my God, I will give you thanks forever!"

Psalm 30:11-12

Darkness

Darkness is disorienting; focusing is difficult
Poor judgment is made when we can't see
Sin blinds our vision; it blinds our entire being

We can only see what's close at hand
We don't see the consequences
that lurk around the bend

We can overcome every obstacle
when we allow Jesus to guide our lives
Jesus doesn't tempt—He'll never try
He keeps us away from difficulties and pride

He hears each cry and dries each tear
His truth adheres to what once was unclear
He removes the blinders that once covered sin
Jesus lights our way, as there is no darkness in Him

It's amazing how clearly we're able to see
when our focus is put on living for Eternity
There's no room for darkness—Only the Lord
We're no longer blinded—Our sight is restored

"I have come as a light to shine in this dark world, so that all who put their trust in me will no longer remain in the dark."

John 12:46

And remember, when you are being tempted, do not say, "God is tempting me." God is never tempted to do wrong, and he never tempts anyone else.

James 1:13

Day Too Late

Do you put things off you feel you should entertain?
Do you say, "Maybe tomorrow; I just can't do it today?"
Do you have any pressing matters in the back of your mind?
Could one possibly be engaging in a relationship with Jesus Christ?

Please don't allow another day to be lost if that's the case
Jesus is the answer to *every* problem you'll ever face
Jesus is a promise keeper—He'll never lead you astray
and He's *always* just a thought or a simple prayer away

When Jesus is in the forefront instead of the rear
our hearts and thoughts become very clear
We can let go of things that aren't heaven-sent
and better live life the way it was meant

Our thoughts, words, and works will be redirected
It's without His presence that we get disconnected
We'll choose to thank and praise the Almighty King
Who intervened on our behalf to set us perfectly free

Today's a new day; it's yesterday's tomorrow
but once it's gone, it can't be borrowed
There are many variables that aren't in our control
as life is filled with joy, uncertainty, and sorrow

But nothing compares to the sorrow there will be
when we want Jesus, but He says, "Away from Me"
There are some things that just can't wait another day
One thing is certain: you don't want to be a day too late!

You must warn each other every day, while it is still "today," so that none of you will be deceived by sin and hardened against God.

Hebrews 3:13

The Deceiver

It's in drugs, music, and vulgarity
In immodest apparel and ungodly speech
Sexual looseness and lust are off the chart
It knows the ways to break God's heart

God destroyed Sodom and Gomorrah
for sexual perversion and immorality
It was a warning sign; do we take heed?
God knows best; do we keep testing?

It's the root of greed, jealousy, and fame
It'll try anything; it's a master at its game
It thrives on resentment, anger, and pride
It's a chameleon and loves to disguise

The devil tried his best to tempt Jesus
and won't think twice to throw us under the bus
his force is strong but not stronger than us
not when it's in the Lord that we trust

The enemy is a master deceiver
Will we fall for it, hook, line and sinker?
Will we allow sin to be used as bait
or get tired of being the catch of the day?

We'll never be able to escape the sin in our lives
until we make the decision to follow Jesus Christ
When we truly follow Jesus and are anchored in Him
there will be no contradictions in the way that we live

"Prove by the way you live that you have repented of your sins and turned to God."

Matthew 3:8

18

Do Unto Others

If we did unto others as we would have them do unto us—
There wouldn't be racism or starvation or violence or wars
There wouldn't be discrimination or neglect toward the poor
There wouldn't be nursing homes filled with filth and abuse
There wouldn't be prisons that further demean the accused

There wouldn't be bullying, cliques, status, or greed
There wouldn't be muggings, shootings, or stabbings
There wouldn't be fighting; there wouldn't be crime
There wouldn't be any "all about me" or "all mine"

Surely you don't want to be robbed
or shot and found dead in a parking lot
or starving or going without water or heat—
All that would exist would be love, joy, and peace

Jesus gave a command before He left the earth
which is to love one another as He has loved us first
The Golden Rule and Great Command go hand in hand
Do unto others as you would have them do unto you
and love one another as Christ Jesus loves you

If you knew the way you treated others
is also the way you treat Almighty God
would you excel in treating others
the way that God has taught?

"So now I am giving you a new commandment: Love each other. Just as I have loved you, you should love each other. Your love for one another will prove to the world that you are my disciples."

John 13:34-35

"Do to others whatever you would like them to do to you. This is the essence of all that is taught in the law and the prophets."

Matthew 7:12

The Final Judgement
Matthew 25:31-46

Do You Ever Wish Someone Would Call?

You went out on a limb for someone
It was really a sacrifice for you
You put in your blood, sweat, and tears
but haven't heard from them in years

It took planning and dedication
It took hours of your time
It cost you dearly
but didn't cost them a dime

Do you ever wish that someone would call?
Do you think that's how the Lord feels, too?
I'd venture to say the answer is yes
He'd love to hear of our gratefulness

If you say you're too busy and the day just slips by
I'm pretty sure that's not a valid excuse in His eyes
We sure find time for all the things we want to do
The Lord doesn't deserve such neglectful abuse

Jesus is the epitome of brotherly love at its best
He paid the penalty for our sins, and we get blessed
Jesus rescued us from the evil world in which we live
He sacrificed His body to shed His blood to cover sin

If the Lord hasn't heard from you lately, please don't delay
Time spent with Him brings true meaning to each new day
The Creator makes it easy for us to send thoughts His way
with minds uniquely wired to reach His throne of grace

Jesus gave his life for our sins, just as God our Father planned, in order to rescue us from this evil world in which we live.

Galatians 1:4

Dormant

We aren't perfect, but when we choose to live for Christ
we'll want to do things that are pleasing in His sight

Our sinful desires will fade away
as the joy of the Lord becomes our strength

Undesirable things are smothered and can't grow
It's like not having any yeast for the dough

The sin in our life is dormant when we live for Christ
The enemy can try, but our account is declined

Resist the enemy so that he becomes weak
Draw close to the King so that sin can sleep

So let us celebrate the festival, not with the old bread of wickedness and evil, but with the new bread of sincerity and truth.

1 Corinthians 5:8

The Drive

If your life is unfulfilled
or in turmoil, it's the perfect time
to turn over the keys and let Jesus drive
He knows the way because He is the Way

He'll take off the brake and get you out of park
Hate will no longer be a force within your heart
He'll remove the roadblocks that hinder your sight
He'll take them out in the flash of an eye

If you're low on fuel or keep stalling out
Jesus fills and ignites all who follow His route
His kindness paves the way to a life of repentance
to a path of inner cleansing that heals and refreshes

Jesus is the only way
to the road of eternal life
He turns around what seems impossible
as He takes you for the ride of your life

Oh, what a glorious day
when you're at your final destination
and because of His great sacrifice
you'll be living in eternal gratification

Unless you didn't fill up when you had the chance
You rejected the sacrifice of this heavenly Man
You chose a wrong turn by dismissing His direction
You chose the path that led to eternal separation

Jesus told him, "I am the way, the truth, and the life. No one can come to the Father except through me."

John 14:6

Epitaph

Time's up!
What will your epitaph read?
How do you want to be remembered?
Is it reflected in the life you lead?

Are you filled with hate, vulgarity, or violence?
Are you greedy, and do you have a restless soul?
Or are you filled with love, joy, charity, and peace
with gentleness, goodness, and self-control?

If Jesus wrote your epitaph
what would He write if you died today?
If it's not how you want to be remembered
He's more than happy to help you change

Jesus Christ is your Savior and King
He fills you with everything that you'll ever need
He grants forgiveness—He takes all of your blame
He gives you peace and takes all of your shame

If you think giving your life to Jesus makes you seem weak
Please think again—It's the opposite; you're being deceived
Jesus Christ is the strongest man that ever walked the earth
Walking with Him will strengthen and give you new birth

When you keep your eyes on Jesus, God's begotten Son
Your priorities and direction shift, and the race will be won
There's no room for hatred, murder, greed, or such things
Only love and respect for the One whose blood washes you clean

Therefore ... let us strip off every weight that slows us down, especially the sin that so easily trips us up. And let us run ... the race God has set before us ... keeping our eyes on Jesus ... who initiates and perfects our faith.

Hebrews 12:1-2

Examine My Heart

Dear God,
I can only imagine the hurt You feel
when we speak so falsely against one You love

Such words come straight from the beast
a vulture devouring the grandest of feasts

Who are we to think we can be so cruel?
Your language, Lord, is like fine jewels

Examine my heart; purge the venom in me
I'm tired of being used as his weaponry

May my words lift up and not tear apart
Please store Your words within my heart

If You wouldn't say something, nor should we
May Your love be extended in the words we speak

May the words of my mouth and the meditation of my heart be pleasing to you,
O LORD, my rock and my redeemer.

Psalm 19:14

Examples

I'd say for the most part that we all love our kids
Are we showing them by the way that we live?
Are we living according to the Lord's direction?
Do we teach that we are His treasured possessions?

Do we trust God with all our heart, mind, and strength?
Do they hear us singing and giving the Lord praise?
Do we live a life of integrity or hide the things we do?
Do we say, "Do as I say; don't do as I do?"

Do we teach that wisdom and discernment are key
and that one day we'll be in the presence of the King?
Do we teach that our hope and faith is in Him
and that Jesus gave up His life for our sins?

Do we teach that we'll all stand in front of the Judge
and be forgiven as we forgive and judged as we judge?
Do we take them to church and teach them to tithe?
Do we teach about fasting, prayer, and sacrifice?

Are we teaching them to focus on the outside
or that the outside reflects what's in our heart?
Do we teach that the enemy is a master deceiver, and
that if God wouldn't think, say, or do it, we shouldn't either?

Are we doing everything we can to fill their souls?
Are we putting forth our best effort if truth be told?
If God Almighty says something, that's what He does
Dear Lord, help us be a pleasing example for our young

Fathers, do not provoke your children to anger by the way you treat them. Rather, bring them up with the discipline and instruction that comes from the Lord.

Ephesians 6:4

Exonerated

If your past holds regrets and you'd like to start anew
there is One who specializes in making such come true
Jesus left His royal throne to take the stand in your place
He assumed full responsibility for every sin you'd ever make

Jesus takes off your shackles and throws away the keys
He died a criminal's death, enabling you to be set free
Your sentence is pardoned and restitution is fully paid
All offenses are expunged for every time you've strayed

Jesus was the scapegoat who vindicates your soul
He exonerates you and makes you perfectly whole
His holy blood was shed in exchange for every crime
as He willingly surrendered with His arms lifted high

Jesus defeated the deadly sting of sin brought on by man
so that you can live in glory in a world that has no end
Your past is covered in righteousness by His saving grace
as Jesus grants acquittal for all who call upon His name

Jesus went to great extremes to purify your soul
There is nothing more important; your soul is pure gold
Jesus is the holy sacrifice enabling you to be as clean as He
What an honor to be deemed innocent in the eyes of the King

Justice declares that you are valued in His sight
as His heavenly court makes each wrong right
Jesus is your Judge, your Jury, and your very Best Friend
He is Powerful, He is Magnificent—He is the Great I AM!

Dear friends, if we deliberately continue sinning after we have received knowledge of the truth, there is no longer any sacrifice that will cover these sins.

Hebrews 10:26

Father, Please Forgive Me

Father, please forgive me
for the things I'm not proud of
Father, please help me feel
that I deserve Your endless love

Help me forgive myself
Grant me the strength to persevere
Help me remember that I'm part of You
and that You hold me very dear

You hate sin, but You love me
Please help me love myself, too
I've made so many mistakes
I am nothing without You

There are many reminders of things that I've done
so I'll focus on the person who I have become
The enemy's strategy is to keep feeding me doubt
I'll just give You more praise and turn that around

I've confessed and repented
All my stains are erased
My slate is washed clean
by Your mercy and grace

Thank You, Lord God, for being my Savior
and rescuing me from my past behavior
Thank You for knowing my repentant heart
and for giving me a brand-new start

"But the tax collector ... beat his chest in sorrow, saying, 'O God, be merciful to me, for I am a sinner.' I tell you, this sinner, not the Pharisee, returned home justified before God."

Luke 18:13-14

Final Sacrifice

Jesus Christ, the Sacrificial Lamb
destroyed all sin created by man
It is finished—the debt is paid
The final sacrifice for sin was made

Jesus defeated our sin with His Holiness
as He was crucified on a wooden beam
He resurrected—His Temple rebuilt
just as He predicted it would be

Jesus took on bodily form
to be the holy sacrifice for sin
Once and for all, sin was perfectly cleansed
There's no need for a sacrifice to be offered ever again

We'll never have to know what it feels like
to have spikes driven through our hands and feet
We'll never have to feel the torture and pain
Jesus paid the price for you and for me

No more animals as atonement for sin
Jesus gave His all—Are you giving your all for Him?
Jesus gave us the best gift that could ever be given
He sacrificed His life for us so our sin could be forgiven

The final sacrifice for sin was made
Thank You, Lord Jesus, for my debt that You paid
Thank You for Your love and for Your forgiving grace
I will forever praise Your holy and mighty name!

That is why, when Christ came into the world, he said to God, "You did not want animal sacrifices or sin offerings. But you have given me a body to offer."

Hebrews 10:5

First Fruit

The fruit on the tree in Eden exposed sin
as it held the source of death

The fruit on the tree on Calvary covered sin
as it held the source of life

God gave us His only begotten Son
He gave Jesus as His first fruit to every single one

What an honor and a privilege to be given such a gift
Please don't let Jesus be the Gift that you dismiss

God cared so much that He sent His very best
He sent His only Son so that we'd all be blessed

When you give, do you give the best in all you do?
Do you follow the Father's example and give your first fruits?

"A tree is identified by its fruit. If a tree is good, its fruit will be good. If a tree is bad, its fruit will be bad."

Matthew 12:33

First Move

Our feelings get hurt; we feel attacked
We feel like we just got stabbed in the back
What once was union is now division and space
We wonder, "What in the world just took place?"

Is there anyone you'd consider calling today
or writing a letter to in order to smooth the way?
Do you need to be the one to make the first move?
Has there been enough time to heal the wounds?

Wouldn't it feel better to get the "whatever" off your chest?
Can you just say, "I think of you often and wish you the best?"
Wouldn't that be better than an awkward random meeting
where you're not sure what to say or do?

Wouldn't a hug be better than having a fight?
Wouldn't peace be better than hatred filling the room?
We don't know what tomorrow holds; I hope it's not regret
I pray for strength for you to say whatever needs to be said

Separation and disagreement are not a pretty tune
Estrangement furthers dissension; it never heals the wounds
Forgiveness is a one-time deal, but bitterness goes on and on
You're bottled up, ready to erupt, or free as a new day's dawn

Please don't allow anger or bitterness to become the norm
When we're resentful and unforgiving, the enemy scores
Whether the issues lie within your family or friends
love as Jesus does; that you'll never regret

Some things are quite serious and will take some time to mend
but for *your* sake, please forgive as Jesus Christ commands

"If you forgive those who sin against you, your heavenly Father will forgive you.
But if you refuse to forgive others, your Father will not forgive your sins."

Matthew 6:14-15

Followers

If you had lived in days of old
and saw Jesus walk in the flesh
If you had witnessed Him feeding thousands
with five loaves and two small fish

If you had seen the lame walk and the blind see
the deaf hear and the dumb speak
If you had seen Lazarus rise from the grave
would you have believed?

Would you have been His follower
if you had seen with your own eyes?
Or would you have been a Doubting Thomas
and wanted proof of the wound in His side?

If Jesus had said, "Follow Me," would you have taken the steps
or walked away from His invitation and forgotten you ever met?
Where are you today? Do you have faith, or do you doubt?
Are you uncertain like a wave, all blown and tossed about?

Doubting is like being unstable in all we say and do
It's a poisonous path that never leads to the truth
If the road we travel doesn't include following Christ
we'll never find the road that leads to eternal life

His holy footsteps guide us to the Father's throne
They illuminate the path that takes us safely home
Do you know the One who says, "Come, Follow Me?"
If not, I encourage you to accept Jesus as your Lord and King

The LORD is good and does what is right; he shows the proper path to those who go astray. He leads the humble in doing right, teaching them his way.

Psalm 25:8-9

Forbidden Fruit

Is the fruit you indulge in fruit that brings reward
or is it displeasing in the eyes of the Lord?

There are fruits of plenty and fruits forbidden
To which fruits are you driven?
By which spirit are they given?

Which voice will you listen to?
Which voice will you obey?
Is it from the spirit of life
or from the spirit of decay?

Have you received the Fruit of Life?
Are you living your life for Jesus Christ?
If not, today can be the day to say

Dear Lord Jesus,

I hunger for You and the fruit of Your grace
Please forgive me for the fruits I did taste
I repent of my past and neglect of You
No longer do I hunger for forbidden fruit

My hunger is to please You and bring You praise
You cleansed me from the first to the last bite I ate
Please strengthen me daily; bring me closer to You
May the fruit I savor be pleasing to You

May you always be filled with the fruit of your salvation — the righteous character produced in your life by Jesus Christ — for this will bring much glory and praise to God.

Philippians 1:11

Don't you realize that you become the slave of whatever you choose to obey? You can be a slave to sin, which leads to death, or you can choose to obey God, which leads to righteous living.

Romans 6:16

Forgiven

No one can take what I have from me
God's tender mercy has set me free
I have forgiveness from God Himself
It's such a welcome and precious gift

I had to know what dirty felt like
so I would know how it feels to be clean
The dirtier we feel and the greater degree of our sin
the more grateful we are to be absolved and forgiven

I know I'm forgiven for the shameful things I've done
because my Savior doesn't keep a record of wrongs
My stains are removed; my slate is washed clean
Jesus sacrificed His body to shed His blood for me

If I never get another thing
I have everything that I'll ever need
Jesus paid my price—He gave me life
I have salvation through Jesus Christ

Thank You for each new day and the mercies that lie within
I pray that I'm a representation of You over and over again
I'm so grateful for Your love—It's entirely changed my life
If You weren't with me now, I couldn't possibly survive

"I tell you, her sins—and they are many—have been forgiven, so she has shown me much love. But a person who is forgiven little shows only little love."

Luke 7:47

Forgiveness

Jesus extended forgiveness
the day He sacrificed His life
He extended forgiveness
with His arms stretched out wide

Jesus extended forgiveness
with His feet nailed to a tree
He extended forgiveness
to you and to me

Jesus extended forgiveness
with every drop of blood He bled
He extended forgiveness
with a thorny crown upon His Head

And with all the pain He had
and was still going through
Jesus asked that we be forgiven
for we know not what we do

Do you need to extend forgiveness
to someone who has caused you harm?
Do you need to open up your heart?
Do you need to open up your arms?

Do you need to ask anyone to forgive something that you've done?
Do you need to ask for forgiveness from God's Begotten Son?
It seems absurd to hold grudges, to hang onto things, big or small
Jesus paid for the entire world's sin, and He forgives us all

Make allowance for each other's faults, and forgive anyone who offends you.
Remember, the Lord forgave you, so you must forgive others.

Colossians 3:13

Freedom

There is freedom in confronting what pains us
and freedom in forgiving what cannot be changed
If you say, "I'll never forgive them for what they have done"
Do you realize that not forgiving is sin just the same?

Maybe it's not being able to forgive yourself
that's keeping the pain within
Do you realize that Jesus sacrificed His life
for every single sin?

When sin is repented of and confessed to the Lord
Jesus forgives them, and they're remembered no more
We hold on to things that God can't even see
We're bitter about things already washed clean

There will always be heartache, sadness, and regret
but they need to be remedied with things heaven-sent
God knows your heart—He knows what you need
He'll send them to you if you have faith and believe

We can't move forward until we deal with the past
I pray you find peace if peace is what you lack
I pray you find freedom if freedom is what you need
I pray you're able to release the pain so you can be set free

I will walk in freedom, for I have devoted myself to your commandments.

Psalm 119:45

*"This is the new covenant I will make with my people on that day, says the Lord:
I will put my laws in their hearts, and I will write them on their minds." Then
he says, "I will never again remember their sins and lawless deeds."*

Hebrews 10:16-17

The Gift of Grace

There is a special gift that's given to those who believe
to those who are grateful to behold the gift they receive
A gift with many layers, this gift will never cease
It continues on for the receiver who believes

This Gift is given by the Giver of Life
This Gift is Jesus, the Risen Christ
This Gift is free to all who ask
This Gift is one that will forever last

Jesus is the Gift that keeps on giving
If we're not living for Him, we're really not living
His holy blood and sacrifice erased our many stains
We didn't do a thing to earn this great exchange

Does your life reflect that it's the Lord you adore?
Have you expressed with your voice that Jesus is Lord?
Do you believe that Jesus was raised from the grave?
Do you love Him with all your heart, mind, and strength?

If you haven't embraced this incredible Gift of God's grace
and your inheritance isn't waiting in His majestic estate
I pray that you're only a breath, a moment, a heartbeat away
from repentance and calling on the Lord to be saved

For it is by believing in your heart that you are made right with God, and it is by confessing with your mouth that you are saved.

Romans 10:10

God saved you by his grace when you believed. And you can't take credit for this; it is a gift from God.

Ephesians 2:8

Guiding Light

We become new creations washed by holy blood
when we invite Jesus to take His place from up above
We become co-heirs and will reign with Jesus Christ
We're adopted into His Family and will inherit eternal life

Our souls will rejoice as we make His presence known
We'll sing a new song as we make His heart our home
Jesus puts so much importance on the state of our souls
that He gave His precious life to cleanse and make us whole

The Light of the World has come to give us new life
and He sends the Holy Spirit as our guiding light
The Spirit is our Helper in so many incredible ways
He prays on our behalf when we don't know what to pray

He guides and comforts—He's the voice that speaks
He is our conscience and dwells within our being
The Holy Spirit is indeed a gift of genuine love
a seal of inheritance and a taste of what is to come

We are entrusted with the Gift of His presence
and given the responsibility to care for this Gift
Please, whatever you do, don't sadden the Spirit He gives
Be a vessel who treasures Him by the way in which you live

The Spirit is God's guarantee that he will give us the inheritance he promised and that he has purchased us to be his own people. He did this so we would praise and glorify him.

Ephesians 1:14

He Loves Me

He loves me! he loves me not
He loves me! He loves you!
Jesus showed us, not in flower petals
but in each drop of His holy blood

Jesus loves us so much
that He became sin in our place
His holy blood was needed
the sin of man so great

The blood of Jesus covers sin
He's the Guardian of our souls
His sacrifice is genuine love
It makes us perfect and whole

Jesus displayed the depth of His love
by taking our sins and making them His
Can you feel the love in His sacrifice?
There is no love greater than this

A new life is given in exchange for our stains
Our sins are removed by God's mercy and grace
Yes, Jesus loves you—He proved this on the cross
Yes, Jesus loves you—It's evil that loves you not

The Son of God, the Great I Am
Savior, Redeemer, and King
Yesterday, today, and tomorrow
Forever, His love will be

He personally carried our sins in his body on the cross so that we can be dead to sin and live for what is right. By his wounds you are healed. Once you were like sheep who wandered away. But now you have turned to your Shepherd, the Guardian of your souls.

1 Peter 2:25

He Sees Us

How differently would you live your life
if you could visibly see the Lord at your side?

Would you have done what you did?
Would you have seen what you saw?

Would you have said what you said?
Would you have bought what you bought?

Would you have given what you gave?
Would you have gone where you went?

Would you have worn what you wore?
Would you have spent what you spent?

Would you do things the same as you do
if you could visibly see the Lord
as He is watching you?

We can't see Him, but He sees us
He knows our hearts—He knows our minds
He knew us before the beginning of time

We, too, will be face to face with Jesus
just like the Samaritan woman at the well
I pray you're looking forward for that day to come
If not, there's no better time to live your life for God's Son

The woman left her water jar beside the well and ran back to the village, telling everyone, "Come and see a man who told me everything I ever did! Could he possibly be the Messiah?"

John 4:1-30

Nothing in all creation is hidden from God. Everything is naked and exposed before his eyes, and he is the one to whom we are accountable.

Hebrews 4:13

He Sets the Captives Free

Jesus was persecuted and executed
to remove all of our debris
He is so full of mercy and grace
that He grants us clemency

Jesus took it upon Himself to set us perfectly free
He took our dirty stains and washed us spotlessly clean
His love is so great that He stepped in to plead our case
We deserved punishment, but Jesus stood in our place

We made the mistakes, but Jesus redeems
He surely deserves the title of Redeemer and King
Can you just imagine His Holiness wiping our sin away
as He hung upon the cross to cover our fall and foul play?

Our Savior loves us all without a shadow of a doubt
He gave His life because saving souls is what it's all about
We either cherish His sacrifice and *prove it* by the way we live
or dismiss it and live disobediently and end up losing *big*

Living our lives for Jesus
is the only way to live a truly wholesome life
It is Jesus and Jesus alone who sets the captives free
He's got all the power—His victorious win took back the keys

What Jesus did for us is a beautiful and big deal
It's something that only His Holiness could do
How do you show your love and appreciation
to this King who proved His love to you?

"The Spirit of the LORD is upon me, for he has anointed me to bring Good News to the poor. He has sent me to proclaim that captives will be released, that the blind will see, that the oppressed will be set free, and that the time of the LORD's favor has come."

Luke 4:18-19

He Took the Stand

I know a man, the best in the land
He willingly took the stand for me
He took the stand for the entire land
the day He died upon a tree

Do you know this man, this *heavenly* man?
The One who sacrificed His life to set us free?
The One who carried our sin on His shoulders?
The One whose blood cleansed our iniquity?

How well do you know Him, I ask of you?
Do you say "Good Morning" when you awake?
Do you keep in touch throughout your day?
Does He reply and take your breath away?

Do you think He's *fictitious* and a *waste of time*
and don't believe that He's *holy* and *divine*?
Please know that He is far from fiction—He is pure truth
and today can be the day that makes you brand new!

Repent of your old thinking; let your new life begin
You'll have a clean slate when you ask Him to forgive
Accepting Jesus is the best thing you could ever do
Praise God for sending His Spirit to live inside of you

Jesus insured security the day He died upon a tree
He took the stand for the entire land to wash impurity
Can you feel the depth of His love the day He gave His life?
Oh, what a Savior we have in Jesus Christ!

God has called us to live holy lives, not impure lives. Therefore, anyone who refuses to live by these rules is not disobeying human teaching but is rejecting God, who gives his Holy Spirit to you.

1 Thessalonians 4:7-8

He's Coming Back

Would you be thrilled or filled with sorrow
if you knew that Jesus was returning tomorrow?
Would you be joyfully singing "Oh, Happy Day"
or be on your face, begging for mercy and grace?

Would you be rethinking your views on Christianity?
Would you relinquish all and fall on trembling knees?
Would you be ashamed because life was all about you?
Would you regret not spending time with God in solitude?

If today was your last day on earth, what would you do?
Would you go out for one more fix, last fling, or rendezvous?
Would you shout from the rooftops that Jesus is on His way?
Would you come out of the closet and finally share your faith?

Jesus cautions us to be on guard and stay alert
Guidelines for wholesome living are found within His Word
The Bible contains all the wisdom that we'll ever need
It's alive; it's full of treasure and speaks to those who read

It's written that the sun and moon will no longer shine
That the stars will be released and fall from the sky
Darkness bows in silence awaiting the arrival of Jesus Christ
The Light of the World returns on clouds of snowy white

It may not be tomorrow, but it's a *fact* He's coming back
The folded cloth left in His tomb meant *exactly that*
The Master will return—The King is very near
Are you ready for the day when Jesus Christ appears?

"At that time … the sun will be darkened, the moon will give no light, the stars will fall from the sky, and the powers in the heavens will be shaken. Then everyone will see the Son of Man coming on the clouds with great power and glory."

Mark 13:24-26

Hearts

That heavy heart of stone that you carry
can be lightened and broken apart
Jesus will chisel it away a piece at a time
when you invite Him to reside in your heart

The Lord will mend your torn and tattered heart
He'll sew you together a stitch at a time
You can trust in the power of the Almighty
His love will be your guide

The warmth of His love will melt a heart that's cold as ice
and turn one of arrogance into one extremely wise
The crude, rude mood will no longer take hold
and unforgiveness will feel like a very hot coal

If your heart is hardened or desensitized
or diseased and filled with ego or pride
or hurt or broken or filled with anger and rage
please know that God is waiting to fill that space

It's a much richer life to live
when our hearts beat as one with His—
When they're in rhythm and not opposition
with the One who sacrificed His life for our sin

"And I will give them singleness of heart and put a new spirit within them. I will take away their stony, stubborn heart and give them a tender, responsive heart, so they will obey my decrees and regulations. Then they will truly be my people, and I will be their God."

Ezekiel 11:19-20

Highest of Highs

Oh, Sweet Jesus,
I pray for my loved ones to realize soon
that desperation, struggles, and emptiness
can't be filled without knowing *You*

The omission of Your presence
causes them to seek and crave
They'll try anything and *everything*
to satisfy their needs or make an escape

I pray with every precious new day
that their unhealthy desires fade away
I pray that their desires are to please You instead
and as they draw close to You their souls will be fed

I pray for their desires to become one with Yours
so they're no longer blinded and You're not ignored
I pray that their fix is building a relationship with You
for deliverance and identity lie in Your intoxicating truth

I pray that they'll cherish and follow Your lead
as Your benefits are lasting and not a temporal thing
I pray that their free-will leads them close to Your side
as spending time with You is what makes them come alive

You, O Lord, are the Highest high there is
You fill all who partake of You with everlasting bliss
You are the greatest pleasure; the source of pure delight
You are and will always be the Highest of *all* highs!

Take delight in the LORD, and he will give you your heart's desires. Commit everything you do to the LORD. Trust him, and he will help you.

Psalm 37:4-5

Home Run

Strike three! You're out!
Thank God that's not His ruling
No one would ever get on base
much less make it to *home plate*!

Jesus scored the winning run
through His death and resurrection
He took our strikes—He took our swings
He crushed opposition with His victorious sting

His blood, sweat, and tears
were drops of love on every base
His relentless dedication
was poised in strength and grace

Jesus had no hesitation
about the game He came to play
He made up for the errors of others
with a Grand Slam that saved the day!

The Heaviest Hitter that has ever scored
will be announced with a trumpet's horn
The Greatest Comeback there ever will be
is the Return of Christ, the King of all Kings

But as we wait for that celebratory day
the enemy will still try to pitch balls our way
Thank You, Lord Jesus, for crushing each hit
and for covering every sin that we'll ever commit

Christ suffered for our sins once for all time. He never sinned, but he died for sinners to bring you safely home to God. He suffered physical death, but he was raised to life in the Spirit.

1 Peter 3:18

How Does Your Garden Grow?

Are you on the lookout for devouring birds that want your seed?
From the vulture that doesn't want the News of Jesus received?
From the scavenger that wants your seed so it can't sprout?
The enemy loses the battle if he can't keep you in doubt

Have you removed the rocks of temptation that cause you to fall?
The ones keeping you from a relationship with Almighty God?
The boulders, heavy and many and a nuisance to remove?
The ones trapping moisture so your seed can't take deep root?

How does your garden grow? What do your priorities show?
Is your garden full of fruit because of the praises you sing?
Or do riches and pleasures keep you from praising the King?
Would removing these thorny treasures cause you great sting?

The harvest is plentiful, but the workers are few
How many souls have you led to the truth?
How many souls have you just passed by?
Be fruitful and multiply seems to apply

May the News of Jesus be your loving cry
as you cultivate and fertilize future souls for Christ
Go out as peaceful lambs—Be loving, gentle, and kind
Treat every soul with value—Help them not wither and die

It's more than a privilege to share such Good News
and quite an honor to rescue the lost and abused
May the seeds of God's love flourish throughout
and the seeds of doubt be choked out like a drought

You will always harvest what you plant. Those who live only to satisfy their own sinful nature will harvest decay and death from that sinful nature. But those who live to please the Spirit will harvest everlasting life from the Spirit.

Galatians 6:7-8

I Can't Do This Without You

Dear God,
I can't do this without You
I'm burdened with so many things
This defeat and misery has the best of me

Life is so unfair sometimes
I need Your help to make it through
I'll keep asking, seeking, and knocking
and pray that my desires are one with You

I ask that You touch those around me
They're so full of deceit, hatred, and unbelief
I really need You, but they need You even more than me
Please show them that You're real—Let them hear You speak

You spoke to Balaam through a donkey and put Jonah in a whale
After getting their attention, they bowed to Your will
I'm lifting up Your children and look forward to what You'll do
I rest in the assurance that You *will* come through

You told me to love others—I'm trying my best
Please strengthen me daily while You do the rest
It's very defeating when opposition is on all sides
Holy Spirit, come—You are welcome day and night

"But to you who are willing to listen, I say, love your enemies! Do good to those who hate you. Bless those who curse you. Pray for those who hurt you. If someone slaps you on one cheek, offer the other cheek also. If someone demands your coat, offer your shirt also."

Luke 6:27-29

I Pledge Allegiance

I pledge allegiance to the One
Who was, and is, and is to come
To Him who is and will always be
Jesus, the Christ, the King of Kings

The Light of the World, the Great I Am
The Prince of Peace, the Sacrificial Lamb
The Good Shepherd, the One True Vine
The Living Water, the Bread of Life

He heals, loves, guides, and protects
Disciplines, forgives, fills, and accepts
He hears and speaks and knows my name
It's through Him alone that I am saved

He healed the deaf, the mute, the blind
Walked on water and turned water into wine
He drove out demons and raised the dead
He fed multitudes with a few loaves of bread

The winds and waves obey His command
All authority was His before time began
I pledge allegiance to the Great I Am
as He is the rock on which I stand

My Salvation, Defender, Refuge, and King
My Comfort and Shelter, my Protector and Peace
My Provider and Healer, my Counselor and Friend
My present, my future, my beginning, and my end!

*Therefore, let us offer through Jesus a continual sacrifice of praise to God,
proclaiming our allegiance to his name.*

Hebrews 13:15

If Only

If only I had read Your Word and believed that it was true
I wouldn't have hurt others—I wouldn't have hurt *You*
You gave commandments for my protection
If only I had lived under Your direction

You would have been my only God
There would have been no other
I wouldn't have used Your name in vain
or disobeyed instruction my parents gave

I wouldn't have coveted or stolen or lied
I wouldn't have thought it was alright to end life
or slept with anyone who wasn't my spouse
I didn't listen then, Lord, but I'm listening *now*

I'm appalled at my selfishness and greed to say the least
I wasn't living for You at all—I was only living for me
As a result, poor choices were made
If only I had lived under the direction You gave

If only I had given You the honor You deserved
If only it was with You that I conferred
I've wasted so much time running from the truth
Now all I want to do is seek more and more of You

You are the perfect example of obedience
Thank You for sacrificing Your life for my sins
You died so that I could be holy and blameless
If that's not love, I don't know what is!

But those who obey God's word truly show how completely they love him. That is how we know we are living in him. Those who say they live in God should live their lives as Jesus did.

1 John 2:5-6

If You Knew

If you knew that satan is behind the negative thoughts you get
that he's in the lies and demeaning voices inside your head
If you knew that he's relentless and doesn't want you to be whole
would you want to stop giving him so much control?

If you knew that ploys of hatred and unforgiveness
are amongst two of his favorite schemes
would you continue harboring these
if that put you on the same team?

If you knew that he's behind impurity and greed
and that he robs you of joy and wants you to seethe
If you knew that you're being used and played for a fool
would you want to stop filling him up with so much fuel?

If you knew that the devil is a master at disguise
that he's constantly tricking with deception and lies
If you knew that his goal is to take you down with him
would it change the way you look at temptation and sin?

If you knew that his focus is to get your focus off of Christ
would you start thinking about things in a different light?
The devil longed to be glorified and still does to this day
and since he can't be honored, he feeds on doubt and hate

The best way to repay this evil is with the love of Jesus Christ
Live in ways that honor our Savior, for love wins every time
I pray this sheds light and brings peace to your soul
Living for Jesus is the only way to be whole

Dear children, keep away from anything that might take God's place in your hearts.

1 John 5:21

In an Instant

In an instant, we leave this life
It's like walking through the wardrobe
We're on one side and then the next
Where will we be? Who will we see?

Is it in a place you've been longing to be
with someone you've been longing to meet?
Are you in the presence of God Most High?
Are you mesmerized by the love in His eyes?

Do you long for His warm and tender embrace
or fall on your knees as you shrink back in shame?
Are you full of regret because you didn't believe?
Could the devil, perhaps, be the next one you see?

Jesus made an exchange and became sin in our place
so that we can stand before Him without any blame
Every sin we've committed was nailed into His hands
Each of our sins are cleansed by the blood of the Lamb

Do you hold His sacrifice dear to your heart
or believe that Jesus and all He represents is a farce?
Do you believe that Jesus gave us life by sacrificing His
and that not believing this is rejecting the life that He gives?

Just as in an instant we leave this earthly life
you can, in an instant, give your life to Jesus Christ
If you haven't yet given your heart to God's Son
Please be encouraged to have that one-on-one

And now, dear children, remain in fellowship with Christ so that when he returns, you will be full of courage and not shrink back from him in shame.

1 John 2:28

Inheritance

What inheritance will be waiting for you
as a result of the earthly life you've led?
Will it be one you're pleased to receive
or one you wish was a really bad dream?

We'll all be getting an inheritance one day
It will be from Jesus, the Risen Christ
The Son of God who left His throne
and for us was crucified

Our inheritance is being kept safe
where moths and rust cannot destroy
Just waiting for that predestined day
when the chosen will have no greater joy

The most fulfilling seven words one could ever hear
are "Well done, my good and faithful servant"
If Jesus says it, He means it
You are worthy; you deserve it

If you don't hear those words
you more than likely
won't like your inheritance either
but you can't turn back time

You can be a dollar short
but you don't want to be a day too late
If Jesus isn't your Savior and Lord
you'll never go through Heaven's gate

"The master was full of praise. 'Well done, my good and faithful servant. You
have been faithful in handling this small amount, so now I will give you many
more responsibilities. Let's celebrate together!'"

Matthew 25:21

Intertwined

Intertwined, You and I
I'm the branch; You're the Vine
So closely connected, a blessing indeed
Your Eternal Spirit resides within me

It gives me great comfort
knowing You're close to my heart
that I'm grafted in with You
and considered to be a fine work of art

I couldn't possibly make it through my day
if You weren't able to hear me when I prayed
I'd be lost without You, Lord, truly I would be
I'd be so empty without You communing with me

When I remain in You and You in me
You nourish every cell in my entire being
You prune me so I can blossom and produce much fruit
There's no end to the possibilities when I'm abiding with You

It's when I'm apart from You
that I don't have life and can't survive
It's apart from You that I'm completely deprived
that my cells are poisoned with denial and pride

My choice is You
with every breath I breathe
Intertwined, You and I, together we will be
living in Your Glorious Kingdom throughout Eternity

*"Yes, I am the vine; you are the branches. Those who remain in me, and I in them,
will produce much fruit. For apart from me you can do nothing."*

John 15:5

The Invitation

You are cordially invited to embrace Jesus Christ
His yoke is easy—His burden is light

All who are weary and heavily laden
please know that His rest is a prayer away

Accepting Jesus as Savior and Lord
brings new strength with each new day

He's always available, so we're never alone
When we stay united, He helps carry our load

We're lost without Him—We need Him in our hearts
Once we have Him, we won't want Him to part

It's up to us, but of this we can be sure:
Our present life is but a blur

The sooner we accept His gracious invitation
the sooner we'll become a brand-new creation

We can also reject His invitation
and reap the consequence this brings

Our decision is eternal—Have you RSVP'd?
You are personally invited to embrace the Great King!

"Come to me, all of you who are weary and carry heavy burdens, and I will give you rest. Take my yoke upon you. Let me teach you, because I am humble and gentle at heart, and you will find rest for your souls."

Matthew 11:28-29

The Judge

Are you angry or hurt over what's happened to you
or maybe believing something you only assume to be true?
Are we so self-righteous to think we deserve to hold a grudge?
Can we just let the past be the past and move forward in love?

When we confess to the Lord, it's remembered no more
If only we could be more like the Lord
Any hurt committed was against God more than us
If God forgives, forgive we must

The enemy knows that loving and forgiving
are things the Lord commanded us to do
he wants us to hold on to the negative
he'll do anything not to lose

It's a game to him, and we're his pawn
Turn the tables and bring on a new dawn
You're the only one that can complete this task
Are you ready to let go of the past?

Is there someone you need to forgive today
over something that may be very trivial by the way?
Is there someone with whom amends need to be made
before something happens and it's way too late?

Can we let the past be the past and move forward in love?
Can we let the Lord be the Lord and let Him be the Judge?
If we're judged as we judge and forgiven as we forgive
is holding on to unforgiveness worth the risk of this?

God alone, who gave the law, is the Judge. He alone has the power to save or to destroy. So what right do you have to judge your neighbor?

James 4:12

For you will be treated as you treat others. The standard you use in judging is the standard by which you will be judged.

Matthew 7:2

Just Not That Into You

It's very obvious by the way that some live
that they are just not that into You
That phrase just hit me like a ton of bricks
I hurt for You, Lord; it really made me sick

The only reason to live is for You
So many people just don't have a clue
They don't need You at present
but they'll sure find You when they do

Numerous distractions push You aside
So many other things to do with our lives
Reading the Bible and getting to know You
is the farthest thing from so many minds

I hurt for You, Lord; I hurt for them, too
Work, errands, and activities come before You
Sunday morning service doesn't even make the list
when shopping and sleeping in can take the place of this

I pray for repentance; this should not be the norm
You deserve to be given our time and adored
I pray that You are the lifestyle we choose, and
that You are included in the things that we do

I pray the distractions that once pushed You aside
will become less important in our daily lives
and that the things we choose to fill our days
will be things that please You and bring You praise

And now, dear brothers and sisters, one final thing. Fix your thoughts on what is true, and honorable, and right, and pure, and lovely, and admirable. Think about things that are excellent and worthy of praise.

Philippians 4:8

Keeper of the Key

There is one key that opens the door of life
This key is Jesus, the Risen Christ
He's patiently waiting with His arms open wide
and on His door is a "Welcome" sign

Do you know the Keeper who holds this key
the One who gave His life for you and for me?
Do you know that His love for us is so great
that He sacrificed His sinless life in our place?

Jesus wants us to feel the depth of His love
He doesn't want anyone to be condemned
Jesus came to reconcile the world
and to call sinners to repent

Jesus is the key to our present
and holds the key to our final destination
Where will you go when your earthly life is over?
Will you be pleased or be wanting a do-over?

I pray it's with the One who holds this key
that you'll be living with Jesus, the King of all Kings
I pray that you'll be in the realm where the Keeper dwells
and not living with regret in the pit and depths of hell

Please know that living for Jesus is fulfilling, fun, and clean
If you don't know this, you're either being prideful or deceived
It's never a dull life with Jesus—He speaks in so many ways
The God of Creation adores you and loves to communicate

*"This is the message from the one who is holy and true, the one who has the key
of David. What he opens, no one can close; and what he closes, no one can open."*

Revelation 3:7

Leper

Some feel they can't come to Jesus
because their pasts are so stained
They're embarrassed and so ashamed

That's the first step; It's a good thing
Jesus is waiting for us to be remorseful
to feel the guilt and shame

Jesus came to call sinners to repent
so repent while time is still at hand
Live your life for this holy man

I was as a leper but covered in sin
It didn't show on the outside
but was consumed within

I asked for forgiveness
and forgiveness I received
I felt healing instantaneously

Thank You, Lord Jesus
for saving a leper like me, and
for sacrificing Your life to make me clean

Thank You for Your love
It's removed scores of painful sores
It's You and *only* You that I honor and adore

One of them when he saw that he was healed, came back to Jesus, shouting, "Praise God!" He fell to the ground at Jesus' feet, thanking him for what he had done ... Jesus asked, "Didn't I heal ten men? Where are the other nine?" ... And Jesus said to the man, "Stand up and go. Your faith has healed you."

Luke 17:15-19

Lies

A lie is an untrue statement with intent to deceive
Does this sound like you; do you ever mislead?
The opposite is truth, a life filled with integrity
What do your words say about the life you lead?

Do you ever cheat to justify the means?
Do you make promises you don't intend to keep?
Do you manipulate, exaggerate, or color the truth?
None of these options are an acceptable excuse

Do you tell lies to make yourself sound cool
but when the truth comes out, you feel like a fool?
Do you have a hard time keeping the lies straight?
The deceiver loves it when we take the bait

We'll never be happy or be at peace
until our hearts are beating with honesty
A fib, a big fat lie, or a white lie in between
we'll all be judged for every idle word we speak

Lying is a dangerous game
and goes against a command God gave
The devil is a deceiver; don't be one, too
Life is so much better when we just tell the truth

Don't be a liar; be trustworthy and refined
Live the truth, the whole truth, and nothing but the truth
Kill the spirit of deceit that comes from the father of lies
Live with complete honesty; live your life like Jesus Christ!

"And I tell you this, you must give an account on judgment day for every idle word you speak. The words you say will either acquit you or condemn you."

Matthew 12:36-37

Lifeline

Are you surrounded by deep water?
Do you feel like you're going to drown?
Have you called on Jesus to save you?
Do you know He'll never let you down?

Jesus will give you a helping hand
He'll reach down into the depths of the sea
His loving arm will pull you up to safe ground
He is your refuge and strength when you're weak

Jesus is your pilot, compass, dinghy, ladder, and rope
He is your transport and safe harbor—He's your great hope
Jesus is your lighthouse—He warns you of dangers ahead
He's your tower of strength and protects you from being misled

Trust that He's always accessible and ready to assist
He guides and navigates and rescues you from the abyss
It's a choppy ride without Jesus on deck—We tend to sink in sin
But it's quite enjoyable when our eyes are focused directly on Him

There'll be no more sinking or floating adrift
There's never a reason to abandon His ship
Don't get distracted like Peter with fear
The Lord is your anchor and ever so near

Jesus is your complete lifeline
He supplies everything you'll ever need
"Take courage—Don't be afraid"
"Ye of little faith, Please, keep your eyes on Me!"

Therefore, we who have fled to him for refuge can have great confidence as we hold to the hope that lies before us. This hope is a strong and trustworthy anchor for our souls.

Hebrews 6:18-19

Lifetime Guarantee

Jesus wants us to know how important we are
He sacrificed His life—He went that far
Jesus proved His love, becoming sin in our place
on that holy Friday, a day of great grace

Jesus is our friend—He is not our foe
He's the only One who died to save our souls
He cleanses our impurity and washes us white as snow
He's the only One who can make us truly whole

We aren't promised a new tomorrow
but we are promised that Jesus
is the Truth, the Life, and the Way

With Him, there is a lifetime guarantee
A life of fulfillment, joy, and peace
Eternal life with the King of Kings

Without Him, the opposite applies
Eternal weeping and gnashing of teeth
Darkness and doom is the life that is reaped

Jesus shed His precious blood for you and for me
There is no greater love than that of Calvary
God loved the world so much that He sent His only Son
All who live for Him will live in His Kingdom come

"There is no greater love than to lay down one's life for one's friends."

John 15:13

Lifetime Sentence

I've made poor choices
and paid *dearly* for my crime
My choices affected many
if I could, I'd turn back time

Society sees me as a loser
and a form of pure scum
I see it in the stares
the judgement, and the shuns

My remorse is great
God Almighty knows this is true
If only people could see
what God sees in me and you

I'm labeled, and I'm an outcast
for the way I used to live
I'm not who I used to be
but people refuse to forgive

I've paid my debt to society
I've done the time for my crime
but so many people still hold this debt
with a lifetime sentence over my head

I'm excluded from employment
Convicted felons need not apply
My past is my past
but it's how I'm defined

Once a loser, always a loser
These are the things that people say
I hear that I have nothing to offer
and that I'm not welcome in their space

People can't see that my heart's been changed
that I've repented and confessed my shame
So many judge my past and hold a bitter grudge
I've been released, but my time's really just begun

There are limitations everywhere I turn
This lifetime sentence is beyond absurd
Hasn't justice been met
in the sentence I've already served?

Jesus said that we are to forgive
as He's forgiven us
and the way that we judge others
is the way that we'll be judged

So if you look at someone
like they're a form of pure scum
and are holding judgement
for what they have done

If you're harboring bitterness
until they take their final breath
please think about the things
that Almighty God has said

When we repent of our sins and confess to the Lord
our Savior says that they're remembered no more
Thank You, Lord Jesus, Almighty Redeemer and King
for washing my stains and making me clean

"Do not call anything impure that God has made clean."

Acts 10:15

The Light

The Lord's light shines for all to envision
when we allow Jesus to be our sole provision
Things that are honest, selfless, loving, and true
develop beautifully when the planks are removed

With obstructions gone, we can love like Him
We're enlightened and able to see our own sin
Love takes over; hate is dismissed
We want to confess with openness

We trade bitterness in for forgiveness
We let go of things not sent from Him
Our outlooks change as well as our heart
We are transformed into a work of His art

When we place our trust in Jesus
He gives us everything we need
When we live our life for Jesus
He completes us and sets us free

We no longer live in darkness
nor do we live in despair
When we walk in His splendor
nothing on earth compares

The light of Christ was put out for a time
as the Savior of the World became sin
Jesus took on darkness once for all
His light was extinguished so ours could begin

For once you were full of darkness, but now you have light from the Lord. So live as people of light! For this light within you produces only what is good and right and true.

Ephesians 5:8-9

Love

Do you like to hear that you're loved
and appreciated for the things you do?
Have you ever told the Lord that you love Him
and appreciate the agony He endured for you?

Jesus proved His love the day He died for our sin
He loves us more than we can ever imagine
Jesus deserves to be loved and recognized
and sincerely thanked for His sacrifice

I'm being quite honest, so here's the truth
It was easy to thank God and ask for forgiveness
but it was foreign for me to say that I loved Him
I admit it was awkward when I first said this

The awkwardness soon disappeared
and became heartfelt, often with tears
Draw close to Him, and He'll come near
Jesus knows when we're truly sincere

I love You, Lord, I truly do
Thank You for dying for my sin
Sin as numerous as the sand on the beach
Thank You for being my Savior and King

I pray that these words are not foreign to you
and can flow from your heart and lips in truth
Jesus gave His life for His friends; that's you and me
If anyone deserves to hear that they're loved, indeed, it is He!

Come close to God, and God will come close to you. Wash your hands, you sinners; purify your hearts, for your loyalty is divided between God and the world. Let there be tears for what you have done.

James 4:8-9

love letter

You've written a letter to the one you love
You put in much time and detail

You want them to know
how very much they mean to you

That you love them so much
you would die for them

You anxiously await their response—
Will they care what you have to say?

Will they store your words in their heart?
Will their life be radically changed?

Will they care how much you love them?
Will they love you in the same way?

The Bible is God's *love letter*
Will we take the time to read it?

Will we care what God has to say?
Will we love Him in return?

Will we store His words in our heart?
Will our lives be radically changed?

Will we care that Jesus sacrificed *His life*
to take *our sins* away?

All Scripture is inspired by God and is useful to teach us what is true and to make us realize what is wrong in our lives. It corrects us when we are wrong and teaches us to do what is right. God uses it to prepare and equip his people to do every good work.

2 Timothy 3:16-17

Makeover

Bitterness and grudges are heavy baggage
Jealousy and envy don't wear well on our face
Anger, hurt, fear, anxiety, worthlessness, and blame
The list goes on and on; it's a lot of extra weight

When one part of our bodies suffers, it all suffers
Negative emotions can make us physically sick
Unforgiveness and resentment are poisonous
Our bodies take a toll under constant stress

When we choose to forgive those who have hurt us
or forgive ourselves, which may seem impossible to do
We'll find that the weight is miraculously gone
We'll feel like we can run a marathon

If your past makes you feel ugly or
you're burdened and weighed down
Love and forgive as Jesus did
No longer will you be bound

Exchange your negative baggage
with truth and faith in Christ
Your outer shell will reflect
the love and peace inside

Worldly makeovers show off the exterior
Focus on the Lord—Showcase your interior
Be transformed by renewing your mind
A makeover in Christ is the best you'll ever find!

Instead, let the Spirit renew your thoughts and attitudes. Put on your new nature, created to be like God—truly righteous and holy.

Ephesians 4:23-24

Mary Had a Little Lamb

Mary had a little Lamb
whose love is the purest you'll know
and if you follow this little Lamb
you've chosen the path that leads you home

Mary was an expectant mother
just as you may possibly be
I know the circumstances are different
but she had faith—she believed

Mary trusted in God
I hope you trust Him, too
Pray and ask for the Lord's guidance
and if you believe, He will get you through

Your baby can't be the Savior
but he or she is someone very special
You'll never know whom your child will become
if you don't choose life for your daughter or your son

Please know that if in your past the opposite took place
Jesus sacrificed His life for every sin we'd ever make
If you've confessed and repented this sin to the Lord
your sin is forgiven and remembered no more

And because there is a soul at conception
your child is waiting in Heaven for you to arrive
where he or she is being cared for by their loving Father
while you encourage others to choose the precious gift of life

You made all the delicate, inner parts of my body and knit me together in my mother's womb. You saw me before I was born. Every day of my life was recorded in your book.

Psalm 139:13, 16

Masterpiece

Do you know that the Lord
considers us to be His Masterpiece?
Do you feel like a Masterpiece?

If your thoughts, works, and what you say
end up on canvas and in the clay—
Would you like the portrait that you're painting?
Would you like the sculpture that you're creating?

Would you want to begin again with a fresh new start?
You can when you repent and let Jesus control your heart
Ask to be forgiven for the wrong things you've done
Jesus will forgive every single one

When you live for Jesus in all you say and do
your life will be clean; you'll be renewed
The way you live paints the portrait
The way you live sculpts the clay

Are you going to like the finished product
when you stand in front of Jesus
on Judgment Day?

For we are God's masterpiece. He has created us anew in Christ Jesus, so we can do the good things he planned for us long ago.

Ephesians 2:10

Me + You = Everlasting Life

I never want to take You for granted, Lord
I often think what I would do
without a certain someone in my life

How many times
do I think of that person being You?
How often do I thank You for all that You do?

It's taken me such a long time to realize
that You're the most important factor in my life
and I'll only be fulfilled when it's in You that I strive

I can't do a thing without You, Lord
You are the only Way to survive
Me + You = Everlasting Life

Thank You for Your unfailing love
and for every blessing You daily give to me
Thank You for Your sacrifice; in You, I'm made complete!

The faithful love of the Lord never ends! His mercies never cease.

Lamentations 3:22

Missing Out

I didn't listen when people told me—
I pray you'll listen when I tell you
Avoiding the Lord in every way
only brings emptiness to each new day

I didn't realize that what I was avoiding
is what would fulfill me the most
Praise God! I've been diagnosed
I've been touched by the Holy Ghost

I wouldn't be able to make it
without the Lord in my life
He always knows what's best
and He's always by my side

I was trying to fill a void, and the only way this is done
is to stop avoiding and running from God's Amazing Son
It's quite the opposite; We should run with great speed
Jesus fills like no other; There is nothing greater than He

I'm so grateful for the fullness that I've been given
which you can have too if you just please listen
You'll never know how much you're missing out
until you allow Jesus to be what you're all about

Pride leads to conflict; those who take advice are wise.

Proverbs 13:10

Moment of Truth

I purchased an addition for my collection today
I gave it the place of honor centered on the bay
I was admiring the design of this fine work of art
It was such a great find and warmed my heart

The space was filling up with all my favorite things
My collection became a step closer to being complete
and then I heard, "Is there room for true worship?
My child, when will you have room for Me?"

The moment of truth hit like lightning
It pierced my soul and brought me to my knees
"Right now, Lord! Please forgive me; I am so sorry"
I was consumed with making life all about me

"Please don't focus on looks and things you don't need
They become distractions that take you from Me
Look to the realities of Heaven, not earthly things
Limit the things that will become obsolete

I don't look at outside appearance
I look at the core of your heart and soul
So put on your new self and become like Me
Clothe yourself in love, in peace, and tender mercy

Teach and counsel with all the wisdom I give
Do everything you do as My representative
Your satisfaction lies in Me—I make you complete
You won't be sorry when you make room for Me"

Set your sights on the realities of heaven ... not the things of earth. Put on your new nature ... and become like him ... clothe yourselves with ... mercy, kindness ... let the peace that comes from Christ rule in your hearts.

Colossians 3:1-17

My Only Hope

I was living my life on the dark side
The force was stronger than me so I thought
I finally realized that I was just being deceived
The invader does not have control over me

My hope is in the Only Begotten One
Jesus Christ, the Son and Lamb of God
He is sovereign and His love immeasurable
He exchanged His life for mine upon the cross

The Bright Morning Star that leads the way
My Mediator, my Anchor, my Shield, my Strength
I found that His presence was what I was searching for
He was who I needed to be fulfilled and win the war

The pull that was so strong didn't have a chance
I put my trust in Jesus to control and guide my path
Darkness doesn't have the power when I let Jesus lead
When I'm on His side, there's always a reason to believe

Jesus took it upon Himself to make me faultless in His eyes
He forgave and completely covered all the things I jeopardized
Holiness came from Heaven to sacrifice His sinless life for me
If that's not the most giving compromise, what could ever be?

Jesus willingly came to rescue rebels like me
Greater is He and my salvation than all of my debris
Jesus is my Knight in shining armor—He's Royal Supremacy
He is my hope, my only hope—He is my Savior and King!

For there is one God and Mediator who can reconcile God and humanity—the man Christ Jesus.

1 Timothy 2:5

Restore to me the joy of your salvation, and make me willing to obey you. Then I will teach your ways to rebels, and they will return to you.

Psalm 51:12-13

New Home

Do you like your new home?
Is it dark, or is it happy and bright?
Is it a little too warm, or is it just right?

Is there more beauty than you ever imagined
or unquenchable fires and constant cries?
Do you long for the Living Water you once denied?

Are you having more joy than you've ever dreamed?
Do you hear angelic voices, or do you hear screams?
Can you see how people who honored the Lord
are filled with happiness and peace?

Do you long to go back
and live your life for God's Son?
Do you want what honoring God can bring?

If your existing home needs repairing
please do so while there is still time
so that when you arrive at your new home
you'll be in the presence of God Most High

And not where the tormented rich man dwells
begging for temporary relief to cool his tongue
He dismissed what the prophets and Jesus taught
He didn't repent of his sins; he didn't turn to God
He's on the dark side of the chasm
that can *never* be crossed

*"If you only knew the gift God has for you and who you are speaking to, you
would ask me, and I would give you living water."*

John 4:10

The parable of the Rich Man and Lazarus.

Luke 16:19-26

No Vacancy

Please be welcomed, honored, and praised
Be my fill, my guide, my strength
Be my thoughts, my words, and actions
You, O Lord, are my utmost passion

Surround me with a barrier of Your love
Anoint me with Your scent so sweet
I pray evil senses me from miles away
and can't stand the scent of me

Fill me with Your presence, Lord
Consume me with Your peace
Help me forgive like You forgive
Help me be aware of deceit

Fill me with Your presence, Lord
so those I meet see You in me
May my outside appearance
reflect You dwell inside of me

Fill me with Your presence, Lord
with mercy, grace, and truth
Fill me with joy and compassion
with fruit that points back to You

I'll keep asking, seeking, and knocking
and in faith, I believe I'll receive
I'll be filled with so much of Your Presence
that "No Vacancy" will light up in me

"Keep on asking, and you will receive what you ask for. Keep on seeking, and you will find. Keep on knocking, and the door will be opened to you. For everyone who asks, receives. Everyone who seeks, finds. And to everyone who knocks, the door will be opened."

Matthew 7:7-8

Not a Secret

Jesus washed me white as snow
as His blood cleansed me of my sin
Sin that may be too embarrassing to say
Sin that's as numerous as the minutes in a day

I can't thank Jesus enough for sacrificing His life for mine
I can only be the best example of His love that I can find
Jesus gave His life for me; it's everything I'll ever need
He's given me the desire to be His hands and feet

Jesus set the example for me to live my days
He was peaceful and kind—He fed and He prayed
Jesus served and encouraged—He comforted and forgave
He shared the Good News, teaching the way to be saved

The only way to the Father is through His holy Son
Jesus is not a secret—He's to be shared with everyone
Jesus is the mediator between this life and the next
The bearer of reconciliation, indeed He's heaven-sent

God demanded sacrifice for sin and provided the Perfect Lamb
He sent His holy and only Son—He sent the Great I Am
Jesus is valuable information—His news should not be hoarded
If you believe this to be true, don't hold back; pay it forward!

Jesus died to save and cleanse our weary souls
He gave up His life to make us perfectly whole
Jesus wiped our slates clean so we can be without fault
That is if you love Him and have faith in what He's all about!

Jesus told him, "I am the way, the truth, and the life. No one can come to the Father except through me."

John 14:6

Not Alone

Your Presence is undeniable
You're embedded in my soul
You walk with me
You go everywhere I go

I'm nothing without You
You give me the breath I breathe
You give life, not only now
but for all Eternity

Your Spirit dwells within me
You give me purpose in life
You replace the void and darkness
with true love and holy light

I'm no longer fearful or anxious
You are my joy and peace of mind
My trust is in You and only You
I have vision where I once was blind

You are beyond amazing
You provide everything I need
Thank You for the generous gifts
You daily give to me

Your sacrifice has love written all over it
No greater love will ever be known
Thank You for sending Your Spirit
so I don't have to go it alone!

"But when the Father sends the Advocate as my representative—that is, the Holy Spirit—he will teach you everything and will remind you of everything I have told you. I am leaving you with a gift—peace of mind and heart. And the peace I give is a gift the world cannot give. So don't be troubled or afraid."

John 14:26-27

Not It

Are you tired of doing the same old things?
Are you burdened with harmful routines?
Are you tired of playing destructive games?
Are you tired of living with regret and shame?

Next time temptation tags and says, "You're it"
know there is power through Jesus Christ to resist
You don't have to jump at temptation's command
when you're led by God's holy hand

You can be strong for one minute
You can be strong for two more
You did it once and can do it again
The minutes add up in multiples of ten

Enough is enough; call him out on his bluff
The enemy surely doesn't care about us
All he wants is the glory from our sin
and our disobedience gives it to him

Game on! Be in control!
Tag is over—Tell evil you're "Not it"
Don't be taken down by the power of sin
Use the power of the Spirit to win!

*The temptations in your life are no different from what others experience. And
God is faithful. He will not allow the temptation to be more than you can stand.
When you are tempted, he will show you a way out so that you can endure.*

1 Corinthians 10:13

Outstretched Arms

With outstretched arms
Jesus showed us His abundant love
as He hung from His limbs on Calvary

His arms were truly the branches
Jesus Christ is the Tree of Life
He defeated sin and darkness
and brought the world His light

Thank You, Jesus, for Your amazing love
Thank You, Jesus, for Your amazing grace
Thank You, Jesus, for the sacrifice You made
bleeding to death at the stake for my sake

Can you imagine the day you see the face of God
and are welcomed by His warm embrace?
Can you imagine being in the presence
of the One whose love is so great?

Can you imagine the day you meet True Love
and are welcomed into His outstretched arms?
Can you imagine what you'll say or do?
If you'll be ecstatic or fall apart?

How wide would you open your arms
if someone asks how much you love the Lord?
Would they be as outstretched as His were for you
the day He sacrificed His life for yours?

*This is real love - not that we loved God, but that he loved us and sent his Son
as a sacrifice to take away our sins.*

1 John 4:10

Prayer

Prayer is nourishment for our souls
It makes us strong; it helps us grow
It's the direct link to the Lord above
It takes us to Him and His great love

Prayer is a tool crafted by God Himself
It's heavy duty so it won't ever wear out
Prayer is powerful and meant to be used
Please don't treat it as worthless refuse

Prayer is an intimate experience
with the holy God of creation
A one-on-one, just you and Him
in personal conversation

It's truly an honor and a great reward
to communicate with the Almighty Lord
He hears each time we give Him praise
and ask anything using His holy name

He knows us better than we know ourselves
and wants us to know Him before time runs out
Jesus loves us so much that He died for our sins
Prayer is essential to become one with Him

If you've never prayed or thanked the Lord
for the sacrifice He made on your behalf, or
If you're ready to accept Him as your Savior
it is my prayer that you don't hold back

Devote yourselves to prayer with an alert mind and a thankful heart.

Colossians 4:2

Prince of Peace

We're mesmerized by deceit in disguise
We're entranced and enslaved by darkness and lies
We're captivated by temptation, and poisoned by greed
We fall for the cunning techniques of the thief

The enemy manipulates in a spell-like trance
Wickedness is vicious; enticement is enhanced
Evil gloats in selfishness; it's fulfilled in our pride
It corrupts and destroys so many lives

Jesus came to redeem us from the fall of such spells
The Prince of Peace saved us from the grip of hell
His sacrifice alone undoes the damage done
That's why the Father sent His only Son

The holy chemistry in the blood of Jesus Christ
Reversed the curse and brought the world new life
Jesus knew the only way to save us was through Him
His *death* and *resurrection* was the *kiss* that covered sin

Jesus wants us to be a part in His never-ending story
and to live with Him forever in the fullness of His glory
The Son of the Most High overcame death to give us life
His love unveils the darkness with His holy light

Jesus is the Prince who paid the people's debt
He bought our sins through the price of His death
Jesus rules! He represents us! He is our defense!
If Jesus is for us, who could ever be against?

Unfailing love and truth have met together. Righteousness and peace have kissed!
Truth springs up from the earth, and righteousness smiles down from heaven.

Psalm 85:10-11

The Promise

A Bundle of Joy born on Christmas Day so many years ago
graciously came from Heaven to save our weary souls
He is Jesus, the Messiah, the Savior long foretold
the Promise that fulfills the prophecies of old

The Newborn King arrived just as prophecy did say
His mother laid the Sacred One upon the cattle's hay
As much as Mary longed to hold her newborn Son
she placed Him in a manger as a sign for everyone

As Passover lambs were swaddled and laid in a manger bed
it's through Jesus, the Sacrificial Lamb, that we're forever fed
It's through this Gift of Life, Heaven's finest wheat
that life is truly found as His precious blood redeems

This unblemished Lamb and first-born male
is the spotless sacrifice who would take our nails
At birth and at death, wrapped in cloth as He lay
this holy Babe was born, to die, to take our stains

Jesus, the Messiah—The Savior long foretold
the Promise that fulfills the prophecies of old
Emmanuel, Prince of Peace, there is none like You
You are the Promise—The Promise come true!

But you, O Bethlehem Ephrathah, are only a small village among all the people of Judah. Yet a ruler of Israel, whose origins are in the distant past, will come from you on my behalf.

Micah 5:2

For a child is born to us, a son is given to us. The government will rest on his shoulders. And he will be called: Wonderful Counselor, Mighty God, Everlasting Father, Prince of Peace.

Isaiah 9:6

Property of Jesus Christ

I was created by God, the Father of Love
and bought through the price of His Son
Jesus brought me back to the Father
as He obediently gave His blood

My life does not belong to me
It is not my own to do as I please
My body should show I respect my King
The One whom all will one day meet

My body has holiness dwelling in me
Why would I want to contaminate this purity?
Why would I want to speak inappropriately
or not cover up what should be private to me?

Why would I choose hatred over peace
or allow unforgiveness to fester into disease?
Why would I not want to be the best I can be
showing my God how much He means to me?

We're all the property of Jesus Christ
and will be returned to Him one day
Will you hold your head up high
and have a smile on your face?

Or hang your head in shame
because His Word was disobeyed
Will you experience great joy or pain
the day that you are claimed?

*Don't you realize that your body is the temple of the Holy Spirit, who lives in
you and was given to you by God? You do not belong to yourself, for God bought
you with a high price. So you must honor God with your body.*

1 Corinthians 6:19-20

The Prowl

On the hunt, on the prowl
Who can the enemy hold captive today?
Be on the hunt; be on the prowl
Who can you show God's love to today?

Lead by example; live by His truth
Reveal deception so it can be removed
Help the lame walk and the blind see
Follow the Lord and obey when He speaks

You could just be the chosen one
who leads to the release of the enemy's trap
by gently sharing the Good News of Christ
through sacrifice and prayer and standing in the gap

Will you be someone who guides others to the Lord
that He may change their hearts and their souls be saved?
Will you be someone who lovingly exposes the darkness
by unveiling God's truth so the trap can be escaped?

Be on guard! Stay alert!
Help the captives be set free!
They're like a puppet on a string
entertaining the enemy

If only we could plainly see the spirit side of life
we'd be slicing the ties of the enemy's lies
and sharing the love of Jesus Christ

Gently instruct those who oppose the truth. Perhaps God will change those people's hearts, and they will learn the truth. Then they will come to their senses and escape from the devil's trap. For they have been held captive by him to do whatever he wants.

2 Timothy 2:22-26

Stay alert! Watch out for your great enemy, the devil. He prowls around like a roaring lion, looking for someone to devour.

1 Peter 5:8

The Puzzle

Life is like a puzzle
We keep looking for the next piece
How much and what will it take
to make us happy and complete?

We may buy this and decorate that
and then redecorate, because
we found something better
to go with the 'this' and the 'that'

We may be concerned
with the way that we dress
As a result, our closets are full
of things we possess

We put so much importance
on so many different things
that we neglect filling in the piece
that makes our puzzle complete

The many pieces we try don't quite align
and never will until Christ is first in our life
Right before Jesus died, He said, "It is finished"
He accomplished everything He'd been sent to do

There were no gaps—Jesus filled in each space
His blood was shed so that sin could be forgiven and erased
His holy sacrifice was the piece enabling removal of our sin
Does your puzzle include Jesus? He included you in His!

"If you try to hang on to your life, you will lose it. But if you give up your life for my sake, you will save it. And what do you benefit if you gain the whole world but lose your own soul? Is anything worth more than your soul?"

Matthew 16:25-26

The Real Deal

He's the King of Kings
The Ace of Hearts
The Straight Flush
He trumps all

He didn't pass; He'll never bluff
He's not a joker; He'll never buck
He's not a shark; He'll never trick
He'll never, ever, ever renege

He's all in
He's the Bridge
He has a call on your life, and
He will raise you up on the very last day

We live the life that we've been dealt
We choose to either live with Him or without
Is Jesus your diamond? Is your heart full of love?
Or are you angry, carrying around spades and clubs?

"For no one can come to me unless the Father who sent me draws them to me, and at the last day I will raise them up. As it is written in the Scriptures, 'They will all be taught by God.' Everyone who listens to the Father and learns from him comes to me."

John 6:44-45

The Reason for the Season

Do you get dressed up in your Sunday best
to attend church on Easter and Christmas Day?
Is it perhaps the only time that you express your faith
or do you avoid this gathering with every breath you take?

Jesus isn't seasonal; He's meant for all time
He is our spiritual seasoning; He is the Bread of Life
Jesus is the reason for the season, but His season never ends
We either walk with Him in fullness or live with emptiness

Our lives won't be tasteless, bitter, or bland
when Jesus is the fount we keep close at hand
Our cup will overflow, and we'll never thirst again
We're filled with Living Water that comes from knowing Him

When we draw close to Jesus, our tastes and His unite
We savor His desires as we become each other's delight
Jesus provides the nutrients that make us feel whole
He is the yeast rising within that brings life to our soul

Communing with Jesus makes us complete
He proves to be the staple that turns bitter into sweet
He satisfies our pallet, as He spices up each day
It's through Him that we're invited to the most elegant buffet

Thank You, Father, for sending Your Son
Thank You, Jesus, for dying for a sinner like me
I cherish the celebration of Your birth and Your death
and I welcome You daily with every single breath!

Taste and see that the Lord is good. Oh, the joys of those who take refuge in him!

Psalm 34:8

Redeemed

My shame is removed by the Great I Am
My sins are cleansed by the blood of the Lamb
I'm no longer bound—I've been redeemed
My remedy is Jesus, Redeemer and King

Jesus is the sacrifice negating my sin
He gave His life for mine—I'm purified in Him
Jesus gives new life—He gives new breath
The Carrier of Righteousness broke the barrier of death

Once and for all, death lost its sting
The venom of sin holds no power over the King
I'm no longer bound—I'm validated and free
My remedy is Jesus, Redeemer and King

Has your shame been removed by the Great I Am?
Have you been cleansed by the blood of the Lamb?
Have you repented? Are you validated and free?
Is Jesus, the Christ, your Redeemer and King?

Let all that I am praise the LORD; with my whole heart, I will praise his holy name. Let all that I am praise the LORD; may I never forget the good things he does for me. He forgives all my sins and heals all my diseases. He redeems me from death and crowns me with love and tender mercies.

Psalm 103:1-4

Reflections

God's tears
could create a new ocean
for all the sadness He sees
His heart has to be breaking
like the ground beneath our feet

Our world is infected with such evil
It's full of racism, hatred, and greed
It's invaded with lust and selfishness
with immorality, gluttony, and deceit

I hope that when God looks at the world
that He sees more good than He sees bad
He deserves to be given the best from us
He gave us ALL that He had

I don't want to add to the Lord's sadness
I want His Spirit to delight in me
drawing closer with each new day
and being who He's called me to be

I'd much rather bring Him joy
than disappointment or tears
I choose to live in obedience
My desire is to have Him near

I long to see the reflection of God
etched into everyone and thing I see
and I pray that His reflection
is what others see in me

Most importantly, I want to remind you that in the last days scoffers will come, mocking the truth and following their own desires.

2 Peter 3:3

Regrets

My flesh had such a hold on me
I just wanted to escape to numb the pain
I woke up to a new day, but I wasn't refreshed
I was filled with remorse, disappointment, and regret

Regrets are common; they take place every day
but they're great lessons if we learn from our mistakes
I stopped beating myself up; I repented and confessed
I looked forward to the victories that would instead lie ahead

One day it all made sense to me
Realizing my worth helped me clearly see
Jesus sacrificed His life so I could be whole
I was finally able to live with true hope

I was under the influence of the master of deceit
Knowing this magnified the ungodliness in me
I took control and sent the enemy on his way
My issues soon resolved; regrets began to fade

I stopped telling myself that I was a pitiful human being
and started looking at myself the way God looks at me
I relied on God to be my strength when I was weak
as I praised Him for who He is and always will be

I can think of no greater regret than this:
not loving the One who died to show us *His*
I wouldn't want my greatest regret to ever be
not living as a representation of my Savior and King

Let the message about Christ, in all its richness, fill your lives. … Sing psalms and hymns and spiritual songs to God with thankful hearts. And whatever you do or say, do it as a representative of the Lord Jesus, giving thanks through him to God the Father.

Colossians 3:16-17

The Rescuer

It's for my children that I pray today
They need You, Lord; You're the only Way
I pray with every precious new day
that their unhealthy desires fade away

Please rescue them from this dark and torturous abyss
Help them know they can have fullness and forgiveness
You are the Healer; with You, they'll not be weak
Their testimonies, oh, the words they will speak

I'm praying for my prayer to catch up with Your timing
Oh, what a special day when they're no longer hiding
Thank You for Your love, forgiveness, mercy, and grace
I believe I'll see the day these mighty miracles take place

Dear Lord, Thank You for allowing my mother to see
that I'm no longer captivated by the enemy
You protect those that love You and trust in Your name
You shelter and cover; Your holy name I proclaim

Thank You for waiting for me to live my life for You
and for all the prayers said for that to come true
You've given every provision that I'll ever need
Your faithful promises are fully guaranteed

You knew what I was up against and didn't give up on me
How many times did You have to turn Your bruised cheek?
I'm so grateful for forgiveness and all the gifts I've received
Thank You for Your merciful love that came and rescued me!

The LORD says, "I will rescue those who love me. I will protect those who trust in my name. When they call on me, I will answer; I will be with them in trouble. I will rescue and honor them."

Psalm 91:14-15

Respect

I feel so unimportant and betrayed
You promised to love and cherish me
I don't feel special or respected
I want to be the only one you see

Shouldn't my husband be a gentleman
a man refined in thought, manner, and taste
a man that's respectful and honorable?
Surely, that's not the case

As infrequent as it may be
and as harmless as you may think it is
the truth of the matter is that you're lusting
Your eyes are on other women's bare skin

That's not how a husband
shows respect to his wife
or how a man shows another
his respect for Jesus Christ

When the occasion presents itself again
my prayer is that you decline and explain why
That's how a husband shows respect to his wife
That's how a true man acts in Jesus Christ

"But I say, anyone who even looks at a woman with lust has already committed adultery with her in his heart."

Matthew 5:28

Roadblock

You whispered
You spoke—You knocked
but I wasn't listening
I needed this roadblock

The timing was perfect—I needed to fall
I'm more grateful than ever for this wakeup call
There's only one way to turn and it's toward You
You're the only One who can get me through

Thank You for the value You place on my life
and for taking me from darkness and into the light
I've shifted my thoughts on the life that is to come
as this life I'm living is a very temporary one

If I hadn't repented of my lifestyle
I would have ended in eternal doom
My life on earth is the test for the final
and I've failed if I'm not with You

I was so blind to think that I was in control
I was a slave to sin and far from being whole
This roadblock has been a blessing in disguise
Everything I cherish has been truly magnified

The desires I seek now are to please You instead
You are my nutrition; through You, my soul is fed
Thank You for this diversion; to You, my heart is poised
Speak Lord; I'm listening as I seek Your will and voice

*And have you forgotten the encouraging words God spoke to you as his children
He said, "My child, don't make light of the LORD'S discipline, and don't give
up when he corrects you. For The Lord disciplines those he loves, and he punishes
each one he accepts as his child."*

Hebrews 12:5-6

Sacrificial Lamb

God chose His only Son
as our ransom before time began
The sinless, spotless Sacrificial Lamb
was sent to save the souls of man

Jesus knew there'd be pain and agony
and that some would not ask to be set free
but Jesus was willing to pay the price
He willingly died in place of you and me

Jesus experienced excruciating pain
but never once did He ever complain
He asked His Father to forgive us
stating that He would take our blame

Jesus carried our cross and became sin in our place
There is no greater love: He is mercy; He is grace
Jesus lived His entire life in complete obedience
yet treated as a criminal and betrayed with a kiss

A crown of thorns was placed and pressed upon His head
each puncture releasing His precious blood of red
Liquid love was pouring from all His broken skin
Jesus broke the curse and deceit of original sin

Jesus was slapped and spit on
He was mocked and stripped
He was repeatedly scourged at the pillar
and beaten with a lead-tipped whip

Jesus was given a robe for the King He proclaimed to be
and a reed stick for a scepter and knelt before in mockery
Above His cross was the crime for which He was accused
The sign was labeled "This is Jesus, the King of the Jews"

It was nine in the morning when they crucified Jesus
He was nailed to a cross by His hands and His feet
Darkness fell and covered the land
starting at noon and ending at three

Jesus said,
"Father, it is finished—
I entrust My Spirit into Your Hands"
and with that said, He breathed His last

Rocks split—The earth trembled
The sanctuary curtain was torn in two
Finally, many believed that Jesus was the Messiah
and that each word He spoke was the truth

Jesus was taken from the cross and laid in the tomb
He arose on the third day, no longer in gloom
Jesus is seated at the right hand of God
He is the only way—All else is a fraud

Jesus accomplished the mission He was sent to fulfill
He was crucified for our sins on a cross on a hill
Jesus is the Savior sent from the Father above
He is our Redeemer—He is Lord—He is Love

The earthquake announced victory over death
as many of the righteous were raised from the dead
They walked into Jerusalem as a sign to say
just as Christ has risen, so shall we one day

"For this is how God loved the world: He gave his one and only Son, so that everyone who believes in him will not perish but have eternal life."

John 3:16

Seek His Face

If you've been looking for love
but haven't found what you've sought
You haven't searched the one true place
You haven't searched for the face of God

For if you did, you'd truly see
Eyes filled with love and with sincerity
Eyes full of mercy, full of grace, and truth
Eyes full of compassion, full of joy over you

It's when you find this love you seek
that the warmth in His eyes melts all deceit
Your focus is renewed; the old's passed away
The last thing on your mind is going astray

We discover the truest meaning of love
when we find the One who was sent from above
We are magnetically drawn to His grace and His peace
We're enamored by the greatness of the One who sets us free

It's when we don't seek His face
that we go our wicked ways
that we end up in darkness
and sin creeps in to play

It's an easy choice to leave the past behind
once we see the love that's written in His eyes
Remaining humbled and turning from wicked ways
is the only option for all who seek and find His face

*If my people, which are called by my name, shall humble themselves, and pray,
and seek my face, and turn from their wicked ways; then will I hear from heaven,
and will forgive their sin, and will heal their land.*

2 Chronicles 7:14

Selfless King

Jesus said a prayer
to His holy Father for you and for me
He said this prayer for all who will ever believe

Jesus prayed that we'd all be one in perfect unity
and for the world to know that it is He
the Father sent to set us free

Jesus wants us to live with Him—forever
in the glory given to Him before the world began
Can you imagine living with the Great I Am?

Jesus prayed for us to know
that we are loved as much as He
Then shortly after, He was arrested
in the Garden of Gethsemane

Jesus knew what was going to take place
He knew the torture—He knew the pain
but even knowing all that He'd face
He still chose to die for the entire human race

Jesus took the time to pray for us before He was betrayed
and then He sacrificed His holy life to take our sins away
If you've never known His love or what His sacrifice brings
I pray that today marks the day you ask Jesus to be your King

*"I am praying ... for all who will ever believe in me ... that they will all be one,
just as you and I are one—as you are in me, Father, and I am in you ... may they
experience such perfect unity that the world will know that you sent me and that
you love them as much as you love me."*

John 17:20-23

Set in Stone

The Lord said that He is the only God
We're not to have other gods in His place
but we're so driven to consume and do
that these are the gods we embrace

We are to keep the Lord's day holy
and not use His sacred name in vain
These are commandments, not suggestions
His name is not to be spoken like it's slang

We should not bear false witness
or commit adultery, covet, kill, or steal
We are to honor our father and mother
These really are a big deal

These are God's commandments
We'd be wise to take His advice
They're obviously very important
God Almighty wrote them twice

God put these laws in place for our protection
He doesn't want anyone to perish or stray
He is the same yesterday, today, and forever
He is our hope, our salvation, and strength

If God isn't the rock on which you stand
and you feel like you're on sinking sand
Please place His desires before your own
by honoring Him and the laws He set in stone

These tablets were God's work; the words on them were written by God himself.

Exodus 32:16

Then the lord told Moses, "Chisel out two stone tablets like the first ones. I will write on them the same words that were on the tablets you smashed."

Exodus 34:1

The Ten Commandments

1. You shall have no other gods before Me.

2. You shall not make idols.

3. You shall not take the name of the LORD your God in vain.

4. Remember the Sabbath day, to keep it holy.

5. Honor your father and your mother.

6. You shall not murder.

7. You shall not commit adultery.

8. You shall not steal.

9. You shall not bear false witness against your neighbor.

10. You shall not covet.

Exodus 20:1-17

Set Me on Fire

Fill me with confidence, Lord, confidence in You
Set me on fire so the flames spread Your truth
Radiate my heat to warm someone's heart
Fan the flames, Lord, I want to do my part

May my love for You encourage others to love You, too
Ignite me if I fizzle out—Help me guide souls to You
Spark the curiosity within all that I meet
May Your warmth be what they long to seek

I want others to see that You live inside of me, and
to know that You are their Friend and not their enemy
Illuminate my life, Lord; purify me—make me glow
For it's in You alone that I strive—You satisfy my soul

You are the flame of fire that burns inside of me
We are bonded together; Without You, I am nothing
Set me on fire, Lord, on fire for You
Set me on fire so the flames spread Your truth

*Jesus said … "You are truly my disciples if you remain faithful to my teachings.
And you will know the truth, and the truth will set you free."*

John 8:31-32

Seventy Times Seven

I could have been at peace a long time ago
but instead, I chose to do life on my own
I chose to put myself above God's law of love
I dismissed His Word, reaping the benefits thereof

I made myself bitter; I made myself sick
It's with good reason that we are told to forgive
It's not only because we'll be forgiven as we forgive
but because of the harm it does to us within

I could have been living in freedom
instead of in prison in gloom and tears
I've made myself completely miserable
carrying this unforgiveness around for years

It wasn't until I recognized the enormity of my sins
in contrast to the times that I've needed to forgive
that forgiving others became a pleasure for me
It's the key that set me free from my misery

The place once inhabited with self-made wounds
and walls of enslavement that I built are gone
I've replaced them with God's treasure of truth
The power of forgiveness was within me all along

My soul cries out with deep gratitude
Extending forgiveness has such a healing effect
With God, there is nothing that is impossible
I praise Him for wanting me to have only the best

Then Peter came to him and asked, "Lord, how often should I forgive someone who sins against me? Seven times?" "No, not seven times," Jesus replied, "but seventy times seven!"

Matthew 18:21-22

The Parable of the Unforgiving Debtor.

Matthew 18:23-35

❧ III ☙

Shattered

Jesus proved His love for us
the day He suffered and died
He enables us to be blameless
and live a holy and eternal life

When we feel the love of Jesus
and appreciate the sacrifice He made
our lives will be miraculously changed
His love will flow all through our veins

When we're truly connected to Jesus
He'll be our strength—He'll be our guide
We'll be full of love and compassion
seeing things through His loving eyes

There are so many gifts that we receive
when we put our all into living for the King
We'll want to live with humility and truth
leaving behind the old and start living anew

Selfishness is gone—Jesus is what matters
It's like our old life is completely shattered
We won't want to go back to pick up the pieces
Jesus cleansed our stains—He completely released us

Jesus gave up His life—He paid for our shame
When we treasure this, we'll never be the same
I pray that you know Jesus as your Savior and Lord
for it's through Him and Him alone that we are restored

For God has not given us a spirit of fear and timidity, but of power, love, and self-discipline. For God saved us and called us to live a holy life. He did this, not because we deserved it, but … to show us his grace through Christ Jesus.

2 Timothy 1:7, 9

Soul Food

Our bodies need nourishment to stay alive
continually being replenished so they're not deprived
Our souls are like that of an invisible organ so to speak
They also need nourishment to survive and remain meek

If our souls aren't fed properly, the results are poor
The truest way to be fed is spending time with the Lord
He extracts all the poisons as He turns bitter into sweet
He's the breath breathing life into the breath that we breathe

He lavishes abundantly—His provision's superb
He generously fills all who feed on His Word
His nuggets of truth nurture and supply fresh new growth
as each word ingested is more precious than silver or gold

Jesus is our lifeline—He enriches our souls
He is our souls' food that makes us feel whole
There are no impurities within His heavenly blend
He adds the finest ingredients for each of His friends

His Word is like honey on which I feast
the sweetest indulgence that makes my soul sing
Like a grain of wheat, fully grown and threshed
Jesus gave His life to become our Living Bread

No one ever has to be hungry, thirsty, empty, or alone
Jesus is our Salvation and the essence that fuels our souls
His endless provision supplies everything we'll ever need
but we'll never experience this if we don't accept Him and believe

*"The true bread of God is the one who comes down from heaven and gives life
to the world." "Sir," they said, "give us that bread every day." Jesus replied, "I
am the bread of life. Whoever comes to me will never be hungry again. Whoever
believes in me will never be thirsty."*

John 6:33-35

Steps

The first step is always the hardest one to take
Practice makes perfect; we try until we make it
One step at a time, one day at a time
From baby steps to a leap of faith

If we truly want to be successful
Jesus needs to be our Number One
He is so worth our time and effort
Nothing compares to God's great Son

Jesus knows the responsibilities we have
He knows all about errands and demands
He also knows if He doesn't make our list
If you haven't yet, please give Him a chance

You can start by saying, "Hello"
and thanking Him for the beautiful day
Please believe that He hears every word
and wants to hear what you have to say

The more you give Him, the more you'll receive
You'll be fulfilled in a way that you didn't foresee
Jesus is a Gift that you'll cherish and always want nearby
He guides your steps when your vision and His see eye-to-eye

No one else can give you breath
or be the One you see at death
Just think of the steps that Jesus took for you
Oh, when we love others, the things that we will do!

Faith is the confidence that what we hope for will actually happen; it gives us assurance about things we cannot see.

Hebrews 11:1

Strongholds

I wasn't seeking God or His Kingdom first
I wasn't living righteously according to His Word
I finally learned the importance of Matthew 6:33
That's when He supplies me with everything I need

I wasn't allowing God to satisfy my hunger or my thirst
I was living for instant gratification, putting my desires first
I wasn't allowing Him to be my strength when I was weak
I was being selfish, the exact opposite of His selfless love for me

I'm not proud of my behavior
I was ashamed, but kept going back for more
I wasn't relying on God to be my strength
or to be whom I was looking for

It's when I finally ran to Him in my weakness
that He strengthened and delivered me
He parted the Red Sea for the Israelites
and He made an escape for me

I rejoice in the Lord because He is good
His Word reveals each answer to the subjects I seek
The Bible is not just a book—It's so fully alive that it speaks
I'm no longer a slave; my identity is in Christ Jesus, my King

The stronghold that had the best of me is a thing of the past
I choose to believe in God's promises, as they are truths that last
With God, all things are possible—I'll savor this until my demise
He is my strength and my healer—He is the One who provides

Seek the Kingdom of God above all else, and live righteously, and he will give you everything you need.

Matthew 6:33

Stumble

We're being observed from nearby and afar
Our actions show where our priorities are
They reveal a tormented or contented soul
and whether or not we're empty or whole

We'll all give an account for the lives that we live
Do you portray the loving model God gives?
If anyone imitated the things that you do
would they be things that God approves?

Are you copying acceptable behaviors of the time
or living conscientiously and being true to His Guide?
Is there anything you do that could lead another astray?
Could they stumble because of something you do or say?

I can think of no greater accomplishment or wish
than leading someone to Christ by the way that we live
What is your focus? What kind of energy do you exude?
What do you want to achieve? What's your dream come true?

Only God can still the torment and fill an empty soul
Only He can forgive sin and make one perfectly whole
Only He can redeem—He is Savior and Lord of Lords
I pray you feel His love and show respect like never before

Dear God,
Please guide my actions to be pleasing in Your sight
May my words lift You up and draw souls to Your light
Please forgive me of my sin, sin too numerous to count
You are finally my focus—I'm so sorry that I left You out

Yes, each of us will give a personal account to God ... Decide instead to live in such a way that you will not cause another believer to stumble and fall.

Romans 14:12-13

Surrender

Are you tired of surrendering to the law?
Are you tired of being constrained?
Are you tired of living life in a cage?

Lift your hands one last time
Surrender your life to Jesus Christ
Repent of all that's not pleasing in His sight

Jesus knows if you're serious, and you will, too
You'll be sickened of the things you used to do
You'll live for the future, not in the past
You'll dwell on things that will forever last

You may not be confined to a jail cell
but you may be bound and need to be set free
If you're consumed with selfishness, anger, pride, or greed
If you're judgmental, immoral, bitter, or unforgiving

If you're engulfed in ungodly thoughts, actions, or speech
or if you're living for you and not for the One who redeems
Please surrender—We're not guaranteed another day
Jesus is our Salvation—There is no other way!

The night is almost gone; the day of salvation will soon be here. So remove your dark deeds like dirty clothes ... Don't participate in the darkness of wild parties and drunkenness, or in sexual promiscuity and immoral living, or in quarreling and jealousy. Instead, clothe yourself with the presence of the Lord Jesus Christ. ...

Romans 13:12-14

Tamed

Our tongues are flames of fire that can't be tamed
until our hearts and tongues are on the same page
It's a spark igniting our entire bodies in flames
The effect is contagious; it's like a ricochet

Out of our hearts come the words we speak
One leads to another, and we get peeved
The claws come out; the venom seethes
Our words can corrupt our entire beings

Our words are so important; they show who we are
They reflect which force is at work within our hearts
They're stirring in our hearts before they're released
What kind of flame comes from words you speak?

We can't control our tongues until our hearts are clean
Tell the enemy to leave and take the poison he brings
Spend time with the Lord; ask and you shall receive
He'll fill you with loving ammunition when you speak

James writes that if we could control our tongues
we could control ourselves in every other way
Let's work on loving words and pure hearts
"Kill with kindness"—What a great phrase!

And "don't sin by letting anger control you." Don't let the sun go down while you are still angry, for anger gives a foothold to the devil.

Ephesians 4:26-27

And among all the parts of the body, the tongue is a flame of fire.

James 3:6

They're With Me

"He's with Me and so is she
I paid their price when I gave My life"
For people who know and love Jesus
these words will be pure delight

We leave one world, into the next
entirely lost or perfectly blessed
Can you imagine this transitional event?
If you're not ready, it may be time to repent

What is this life when in the end we die
and our final destination is not eternal life?
The only way to have this life that never ends
is to place your life in the One that the Father sent

You won't be giving up anything
when you invite Jesus to be your everything
His presence fills your life with warmth and truth
You're no longer deceived believing life's all about you

One day you're going to want Jesus on your side
but it's impossible if you don't give your life to Christ
Our souls are very important—Jesus died to show us this
Will you be one that proudly says, "Oh yes, I'm one of His!"

*Now all glory to God, who is able to keep you from falling away and will bring
you with great joy into his glorious presence without a single fault. All glory to
him who alone is God, our Savior through Jesus Christ our Lord. All glory, maj-
esty, power, and authority are his before all time, and in the present, and beyond
all time! Amen.*

Jude 1:24-25

Thief in the Night

Jesus sacrificed His life for the sins of all mankind
He's merciful and compassionate—He's gracious and kind
He is the Creator of the World—He's Supreme and He's Divine
He is a loving and forgiving God who wants to be in our lives

But many will doubt God and the promises He's made
They will mock Him and His truth in these very last days
Many will live for their own desires and go their own way
despising authority and ignoring the commands that He gave

We are presently living in these last days and end times
time between the first and second coming of Christ
Some are eagerly waiting for the Day of the Lord to arrive
while others will find it as a most unpleasant surprise

Jesus is being very patient about His return
He's giving us the chance to repent of our ways
He doesn't want any of us to perish or be destroyed
He wants us to know Him and to have eternal joy

His Word tells of the past and the things that are to come
It tells us of the fire that will cleanse just like the flood
This day is unknown, but it will soon come to light
Jesus will come as unexpectedly as a thief in the night

There's no time like the present
to live for the One who gave His life for you
We're either for Him or against Him
Lukewarm will just not do

The Lord isn't really being slow about his promise, as some people think. No, he is being patient for your sake. He does not want anyone to be destroyed, but wants everyone to repent. But the day of the Lord will come as unexpectedly as a thief.

2 Peter 3:9-10

But since you are like lukewarm water, neither hot nor cold, I will spit you out of my mouth!

Revelation 3:16

Thoughts

My life is shaped by my thoughts
Therefore, they shape my entire life
Dear Lord, I pray for healthy thoughts
that mold me and don't cut like a knife

I pray they're chosen carefully
so they lift and don't demean
What a waste of time and energy
thinking about things that poison me

My thoughts are so very important
They're acted out and show who I am
I know You'll never stop teaching me
You'll always lend me Your helping hand

The more time I spend with You
the easier it becomes to be positive and true
I'm tired of negativity; it takes up precious room

If I'm not comfortable, I don't want to stay
so if in me I want You to feel at home
I must choose to keep You in first place

I'm transformed by renewing my mind
I can do this through the power of the Divine
The Holy Spirit will guide me every step of the way
I want to make it welcoming so His Spirit wants to stay

Don't copy the behavior and customs of this world, but let God transform you into a new person by changing the way you think. Then you will learn to know God's will for you, which is good and pleasing and perfect.

Romans 12:2

Tithe Your Blessing

Have you ever wondered
why you're blessed the way you are?

Is it in talent or kindness?
In serving or speaking?
In humbleness or consoling?
In forgiveness or in giving?

Is it through encouragement
or going that extra mile?
Or is it just giving
a genuinely friendly smile?

Do we really comprehend
that everything good we possess
is given by Almighty King?

Are we doing the best
with the resources He's given
or holding them tight within our reach?

If we gave away a tenth of what we own
do you think we would have less or more?
That which we do to the least of our brothers
is that which we do unto the Lord!

"And the King will say, 'I tell you the truth, when you did it to one of the least of these my brothers and sisters, you were doing it to me!"

Matthew 25:40

Too Good to be True

Have you ever gotten a gift that made you smile?
One that gave you new direction and changed your life?
One you thought was entirely too good to be true?
One you didn't know could make you feel the way you do?

One that gives you new breath and new strength?
One better than all the rest—One you could never repay?
One that when given brings life to your soul?
One that surrounds you and makes you feel whole?

We have a loving and caring Father
who gave His Son as this precious Gift
He gave His holy and only Son
as the sacrifice to pay for our sin

Jesus took on the role of Servant
to extend such riches our way
We have a trove full of treasures
when it's in Him that we place our faith

I'm sure you've heard the saying
"If it sounds too good to be true, it probably is"
That's not the case with the News of Jesus Christ
It's the True News that brings the world new life

"This is the message of Good News for the people of Israel—that there is peace with God through Jesus Christ, who is Lord of all."

Acts 10:36

Transformed

His holy body was transformed
as He was invaded by our shame
Jesus was beaten beyond recognition
He paid the price we couldn't pay

Sin is a brutal battle
It strips, it mocks, it lies
It's judgmental and unforgiving
Sin is denying Jesus Christ

His sinless life was given
for the sins of all mankind
transforming us into holiness
to live with the Holy of Holiest

Jesus took all sin upon His shoulders
the day He gave His life away
He's filled with love and compassion
with forgiveness, mercy, and grace

Jesus left His throne from up above
to wear our sin out of His great love
In judgment He stood, making us whole
Jesus is the Savior and the Lover of our souls!

For God's will was for us to be made holy by the sacrifice of the body of Jesus Christ, once for all time.

Hebrews 10:10

His face was so disfigured he seemed hardly human, and from his appearance, one would scarcely know he was a man.

Isaiah 52:14

Treasure Hunt

Our lives are full of endless possibilities
What can we do? What can we buy? Who can we be?

Some do whatever it takes and never stop to think
We put so much importance on our status and our things

If we're not seeking treasures that please Almighty God
our treasures are worthless and will end up in rot

One day we'll realize that we didn't have the best
if we put false treasures in a false treasure chest

We're empowered when Jesus is our Savior and King
It's through Him and Him alone that we can do all things

In your achievements, do you give Him credit due?
Are you looking through His eyes or through a worldly view?

Jesus is the True Treasure above all the rest
and the Kingdom of Heaven is the true treasure chest

If Jesus is your treasure, and you live for Him with zest
you'll have the grandest of riches and be abundantly blessed

For the world offers only a craving for physical pleasure, a craving for everything we see, and pride in our achievements and possessions. These are not from the Father, but are from this world.

1 John 2:16

Wherever your treasure is, there the desires of your heart will also be.

Matthew 6:21

Trials

Darkness has to be exposed
before the light can begin to shine
You are always with me, Lord
You always hear my cries

I am to be joyful over my trials
because they test my faith in You
They develop maturity and perseverance
so I can be complete in all I say and do

I can't do this without You, Lord
The pain is beyond belief
Nothing makes sense
I'm starving for Your peace

There are so many questions
running through my mind
My heart is beating
but I don't feel alive

You must believe that I can bear this
In my weakness, You are my strength
I place my faith in Your promise
You said all I need is Your grace

I take comfort in knowing
that You'll always hear me when I call
and that You're always there to pick me up
each and every time I fall

*Each time he said, "My grace is all you need. My power works best in weakness."
So now I am glad to boast about my weaknesses, so that the power of Christ can
work through me.*

2 Corinthians 12:9

True Man

The most attractive quality in a man
is the respect that he has toward Jesus Christ
It's carried through every aspect of his life
He's not concerned with ego, status, or pride

He makes a great husband and father
He makes a great brother and friend
He knows that life is not about him
He loves the Lord and doesn't pretend

He's not ashamed to have a relationship
with the One who gave His life for him
He honors his Lord by the way that he lives
He's true to his word and chooses to forgive

He waits for marriage; he keeps his lady pure
That's a man who is spiritually mature
He believes in monogamy and cherishes his wife
As a result, he gets rewarded with the quality of life

Inappropriate language and shows
are not things he uses or views
His language is God-approved
and certain places are just plain taboo

The devil knows where to entice with sin
but only has power when it's given to him
An obedient man pleases God's tender heart
If you're not living for Him, I implore you to start

Run from sexual sin! No other sin so clearly affects the body as this one does. For sexual immorality is a sin against your own body.

1 Corinthians 6:18

The man who finds a wife finds a treasure, and he receives favor from the LORD.

Proverbs 18:22

Unanswered Prayer

Jesus said that before we pray
that we are to forgive all things
following His example
holding back nothing

So many prayers are unanswered
Are you harboring unforgiveness?
Can we expect an answered prayer
if God can't even hear it?

If we want to be forgiven
and want God to hear our prayers
We need to forgive as He's commanded
unless "Unforgiven" is what we want to hear

"But when you are praying, first forgive anyone you are holding a grudge against, so that your Father in heaven will forgive your sins, too."

Mark 11:25

Vessel

There's nothing I can do as I look back
except forgive myself for things in my past
I've lost precious time on what I once thought absurd
but I'm making it up, learning truth through God's Word

The Lord always exceeds my grandest dreams
I asked, and I received—I have everything I need
I extended my heart, my voice, and my hands
I've been given new life; how grateful I am

I've been delivered by the Great I Am
I've been set free by the blood of the Lamb
I was a vessel in which sin was displayed
but I've made a choice to leave my old ways

I'm now a vessel that's living the Good News
I thank Almighty God for His Spirit of Truth
My redemption is through the sacrifice of Christ
who obediently gave His sinless life for mine

No longer do I feel like a worthless mound
or that forgiveness could never be found
I have peace that comes from knowing the Lord
Thank You, Lord Jesus, for the love that You bore

*Now all glory to God, who is able, through his mighty power at work within us,
to accomplish infinitely more than we might ask or think.*

Ephesians 3:20

War

We're at war with ourselves
when our hearts and minds aren't at peace
Please don't allow your thoughts to rob your dignity

The enemy wants us to dwell in the past
on things gone wrong and on things gone bad
he loves the war and doesn't want it to end
his arsenal is full of weapons he sends

Life isn't always fair and may not go as planned
but there is comfort knowing the past is just that
I thank God for all the things that didn't happen
but certainly could have

Be like the Mighty Warrior
who fought for our lives and won
Jesus is the epitome of love and forgiveness
He's shown us the way this is done

We have all the artillery that we'll ever need
when we place our trust in the Almighty King
With hearts and minds at perfect peace
the once hostile environment comes to a cease

It's hard to move forward when we're living in the past
Turn yourself around and make beauty from your ash
Take in His breath each time you extend forgiveness or repent
and look forward to your victories in Christ that lie ahead

No, dear brothers and sisters, I have not achieved it, but I focus on this one thing: Forgetting the past and looking forward to what lies ahead, I press on to reach the end of the race and receive the heavenly prize for which God, through Christ Jesus, is calling us.

Philippians 3:13-14

We Can Make a Change

I thought I was cool for picking on his ears
I told him they were so big he could fly
He ended the comments by taking his life
I'm the Dumbo now; it serves me right

My life was so empty I belittled others to feel cool
I wasn't cool at all; I was a complete and utter fool
He lived with ridicule; I live with regret and shame
We're all unique individuals; God doesn't make mistakes

So many people are bullied and ostracized
for their appearances or the way they speak
for where they live or for the car they drive
for their faith, morals and beliefs

Scarred reputations damage lives
Some retaliate or commit suicide
It's a torturous epidemic, and it needs to go away
There are entirely too many tragedies taking place

If everyone gave a dollar to a cause
the effect would be more than great
just as prayer would be if we prayed
for repentance and revival to take place

There won't be room for the latest cruel game
or selfishness, or neglect, or hatred, or fame
The answer is to put God first, not to take Him away
Yes, we really can make a positive and lasting change!

If you claim to be religious but don't control your tongue, you are fooling yourself, and your religion is worthless.

James 1:26

The Web

Do you feel entangled in a web?
Are you a hostage within its maze?
Do you feel an unwelcome presence?
Are you ready to make an escape?

The presence of evil is cunning and quick
It's very deadly; it can make you sick
It creates a work of art and draws you in
It manipulates and entices with sin

You can break free from the one who deceives
You can get out of his sticky web of trickery
It's an entangled web in which the deceiver weaves
but it's in your power to demand that he leaves

It's in the name of Jesus
that he has to obey your command
You have more power than he'll ever have
The web is thread—The Lord is a Three-Stranded Cord

I don't know about you, but I choose the Lord!

When the seventy-two disciples returned, they joyfully reported to him, Lord, even the demons obey us when we use your name!

Luke 10:17

Weight of Sin

How much do you think sin weighs?
Can you imagine the weight Jesus held
the day He carried the sin of the entire world?
How much of that weight belonged to you?

Thank You, Jesus, for dying for my sins
The sins of my past and sins I've yet to commit
Dear Lord, I'm asking for forgiveness, please
My sins alone could bring You to Your knees

I love You, Lord, for who You are
and for what You've done for all mankind
You are the epitome of an obedient son
and the perfect example of true sacrifice

One day You'll get all the honor You deserve
The Greatest Event of All Time
Many will try, but they'll never top You
Oh, what a day to look forward to!

Yet it was our weaknesses he carried; it was our sorrows that weighed him down.

Isaiah 53:4

What Do You See?

Teacher, Teacher, what do You see?
What do You see when You're looking at me?
Are the things I do pleasing in Your sight?
Do my words sound anything like Yours might?

Do You see joy expressed in my smiling face?
Do You see peace flowing throughout my veins?
Do You see love pumping in every beat of my heart?
Do You see comfort extended in my loving arms?

Do You see forgiveness in my eyes and my speech?
Do You see compassion in my actions and deeds?
Do You see patience, goodness and self-control?
Do You see thankfulness for wisdom You bestow?

Do You see me as sincere and chasing peace?
Do You see me following **Your** loving lead?
Do You see me **serving and sharing** Your news?
Do You **see anything in me that looks** like You?

Oh, My Dear Child—This is what I see
I see you diligently being My hands and My feet
Keep up the good work; you've come a long way
Keep sharing your gift; you're doing great!

*Imitate God, therefore, in everything you do, because you are his dear children.
Live a life filled with love, following the example of Christ. He loved us and
offered himself as a sacrifice for us, a pleasing aroma to God.*

Ephesians 5:1-2

Whispers

Will the whisper of sin hold you hostage
or will your desire to please God set you free?
Will you live as a prisoner in the enemy's traps
or rush to God for assurance and peace?

Temptations are an opportunity to run to God
where He's waiting for you with wide-open arms
God is your strength when you feel hopeless and weak
It's amazing what happens when you allow Him to lead

Silence the whispers within
when temptation comes your way
Let scripture be your ammunition
when the enemy attempts to sway

May each whisper of temptation
go in one ear and out the other so fast
that it doesn't have a chance to manifest
Allow God and His Word to be your defense

The enemy is an intruder
an uninvited, deceiving pest
but you get to choose the outcome
You choose to be his slave or decline his requests

But Jesus told him, "No! The Scriptures say, 'People do not live by bread alone, but by every word that comes from the mouth of God.'"

Matthew 4:4

Jesus responded, "The Scriptures also say, 'You must not test the LORD your God.'"

Matthew 4:7

"Get out of here, Satan," Jesus told him. "For the Scriptures say, 'You must worship the LORD your God and serve only him.'"

Matthew 4:10

Wings

Your mother wanted more for you
She made a sacrifice by setting you free
She couldn't give you the life you deserve
but knew someone else could fill your every need

Please don't feel abandoned
or that you're not important to her
The true fact will always remain:
Without her loss, you'd have no gain

It's not that she doesn't care about you
She cares much, and her love is deep
There's an empty place within her heart
yet she can be at peace

She gave you endless possibilities
She gave you more than just dreams
If you look through her heart and eyes, you'll see
She didn't abandon you—She gave you wings!

Even if my father and mother abandon me, the Lord will hold me close.

Psalm 27:10

Wool of Deceit

Can anything that God says is wrong be okay?
Can anything change His "Nay" to a "Yea?"
Can anything that God forbids become obsolete?
Can anything that God has said *ever* take a back seat?

People outright defy the laws of the King
They lie, they steal, they kill, they cheat
What some call victory is really defeat
The enemy has society wrapped in deceit

A wolf in sheep's clothing is his disguise
The wool is covering over so many eyes
Sin is an infectious, debilitating disease
Don't be fooled; please take serious heed

God is God—We are not
Lawbreakers play with fire, and it's hot
It will never, ever, be okay
and will be addressed on Judgment Day

God set boundaries for our protection
His guide leads away from evil and temptation
God is love and holiness and always knows best
He knows exactly what we're up against

If you're being misled or living a life of decay
Please give your life to Jesus—He is the only Way
Jesus shed His blood to cover our *contemptible* fall
He doesn't have favorites—He was crucified for all!

Don't be misled—you cannot mock the justice of God. You will always harvest what you plant. Those who live only to satisfy their own sinful nature will harvest decay and death from that sinful nature. But those who live to please the Spirit will harvest everlasting life from the Spirit.

Galatians 6:7-8

Worth the Fight

You may think you're alone
but it's on every page
It's behind every closed door
and in each and every exchange

When temptation calls and takes control
and we give in, it's reached its goal
Evil draws us in, and we become one
It gets stronger, but we become numb

You are stronger than your temptation
You have the ability to sever the ties
Your help is in the Almighty King
His strength in you is all you need

Jesus is waiting—He's waiting for you
He is the One we need to be drawn to
Jesus is the One who deserves all the glory
Make Him Number One, and see how you flourish

Nothing worth fighting for is ever easy
just like the fight that was fought for us
Jesus sacrificed His holiness for our many sins
because He loves us, and we're worth it to Him

If Jesus can see our worth and endure the pain for us
it's our turn to show Him that it's in Him that we trust
All darkness is exposed by His holy light
Our lives, our souls, are so worth the fight!

Oh, what a miserable person I am! Who will free me from this life that is dominated by sin and death? Thank God! The answer is in Jesus Christ our Lord.

Romans 7:24-25

You and Only You

Your Spirit is so loving and giving
patiently longing to be within
A special prayer from me to You
is where it all begins

I felt such peace when I chose You
With pride, I deem You Best Friend
As a believer, I'm never alone
With You, there is no end

My life of deceit is uncovered
I have Your Spirit as my guide
Your Living Word reveals all truth
You've opened up my eyes

Repenting and confessing refresh me
They're gifts that cleanse my soul
Walking with You and only You
is my priority and utmost goal

Thank You for sending Your Spirit
to reside in and walk with me
What an honor and a privilege
to have a part of Your Trinity

I'm no longer living in darkness
and darkness is not welcome inside
I house the light of the Living God
His brilliance I will not hide

"No one lights a lamp and then hides it or puts it under a basket. Instead, a lamp is placed on a stand, where its light can be seen by all who enter the house."

Luke 11:33

You Are Very Much Seen

Do you feel lonely?
Do you feel unloved?
Do you feel rejected?
Do you feel shunned?

Do you feel useless?
Do you feel unclean?
Do you feel unworthy?
Do you feel unseen?

The Lord knows how it feels to be rejected
He knows first-hand how it feels to have pain

He knows how it feels
to be shunned and unloved
He knows how it feels
to be mocked and called names

Please know this: You're not alone
You are very much loved—You are useful
You are worthy—You are His

And not only are you loved by the Almighty King
Looking through His eyes, you are very much seen!

*Do not be afraid, for I have ransomed you. I have called you by name; you
are mine. When you go through deep waters, I will be with you. When you go
through rivers of difficulty, you will not drown. When you walk through the fire
of oppression, you will not be burned up; the flames will not consume you.*

Isaiah 43:1-2

Thank you for taking the time to read what's been placed in and on my heart. If you've been blessed by what you've read, please pay it forward and share it with a friend. I'd also like to encourage you to consider sending a copy to the chaplain of a *local or state jail or prison. So many incarcerated individuals are starving for the Savior. They need to know that they are loved beyond measure and can be forgiven for their past. None of us can cast the first stone, but we sure can help someone in need. They need hope. They need truth. I didn't mention this in the beginning of the book, but I was also told that what I'd do would have an impact on many souls, but that can't happen without your support. You never know; the book you share or send may end up in the hands of the person that God wanted you to lead directly to Him. It's a win, win situation!

I didn't realize that I had anything to offer, but the Lord set me straight. God surpasses any desire that we could ever have. I asked for confidence to help me share His love and Good News and He's given me this outlet as an answer to prayer. What an amazing God we serve! I pray that you, too, use the gift that has been given to you to further His Kingdom and bring glory to Him and His mighty name.

Your sister in Christ,

Debbie Andrews Smith

echoesofhisheart@gmail.com

*Each facility works differently. All facilities will accept packages from Amazon and legitimate publishing websites, but not all will accept personal packages, hence sending it to the chaplain to distribute or add to the library. More information about facility listings can be found in my marketplace at kingdomwinds.com. Please search for Debbie Andrews Smith.

Made in the USA
Columbia, SC
17 August 2020